THE
COMPLETE
BOOK OF
MOON
SPELLS

THE COMPLETE BOOK OF MOON SPELLS

Rituals, Practices, and Potions for

ABUNDANCE

MICHAEL HERKES

ROCKRIDGE
PRESS

CONTENTS

To the moonchild:
May you glow with abundance!

INTRODUCTION

I came into witchcraft for the same reasons most do—to cast spells, gain control, and create change in my life. My exploration into the magical art of witchcraft was initiated during the growing pains of my preteen years. At the time, I had a robust attraction to witches and the occult, so the desire came naturally as shows and movies started to explore the world of witchcraft. This led me to research and practice, where I learned that there was much more to witch life than what was shown in the Hollywood "reel" world. In the real world of witchcraft, spells were less supernatural and more tangible, essentially acting as prayers that one would accent with energy sources to enhance the laws of attraction. These energy sources could take on a variety of forms, such as candles, colors, crystals, herbs, and even timing—such as that of the lunar phases.

Looking back on my childhood, I was completely spellbound by the lunar rays descending upon me from the black abyss of night. I believed the moon was a living thing and sensed it watching over me like a guardian. On the nights that it was full, I would gaze up and try to make out a face from the contrast of craters and light reflecting off its surface. I talked to it and took comfort from the confessions I declared as I stood in its glorious luminescence. Now that I am an adept witch, the moon has elevated in significance for me. It is more than fascinating. It is magical, glamorous, and a conduit for abundance.

Abundance can get confused with simply riches and material success. Magical abundance is much more than that. It comes from an interweaving of mind, body, and spirit. It is about the joy that comes from manifesting your goals and desires and living a truly enchanted life. There are many ways in which one can strive to do this, but the moon remains a powerful source of energy for anyone, witch or not, to become a magnet for more blessings from the universe.

I've been practicing witchcraft for nearly two decades, and the moon is still a primary anchor in my spellcasting and a continuing source of inspiration. This book will highlight the phases, folklore, and science of the moon while outlining different rituals one can perform to set intentions, achieve balance, and ultimately attract a wealth of this abundance I speak of. Part 1 of the book will serve as a foundation for part 2, which has spells and magical techniques that focus on the areas of love, money, health, success, and happiness. Unlike most books on moon magic, the spells and rituals will be divided into the eight phases of the moon, creating a more dynamic practice for intention and reflection. Regardless of your experience level or the form of abundance you are looking to achieve through your witchcrafting, you will find something in these pages to allow endless and free-flowing abundance in your life. So grab your broomstick and join me as I guide you on a magical journey to the moon!

PRACTICING MOON MAGIC

Welcome to part 1 of *The Complete Book of Moon Spells*! Here we will begin to explore the mysteries of the moon.

Chapter 1 will address the "why" and serve as your introduction to moon magic. We will touch on the historical relevance of the moon, how ancient beliefs have evolved into modern practice, and the moon's overall relationship to the manifestation of abundance.

Chapter 2 will be the "how" and act as a primer on creating your lunar atmosphere for harnessing the moon's power. Here we will examine various techniques for casting spells in alignment with the moon's phases while touching on the different customs and ingredients used in moon magic.

CHAPTER 1

Harnessing the Power of the Moon

The moon has remained an object of fascination for centuries. Ancient cultures from around the world have celebrated it, seeing the relevancy in its effects on the psyche and human experience. As the world has evolved, we have studied the moon and have even walked on its dusty landscape. Today we still observe its splendor: Most calendars include the phases of the moon, there are moon apps for our smartphones, and searching for #moonmagic on Instagram will result in hundreds of thousands of hits. Within the rise of new age spirituality, neo-paganism, witchcraft, and Wicca, the moon has found new relevance today as an energy source for manifestation, transformation, and abundance. Nevertheless, one does not have to identify as a member of the magical community to benefit from the abundant power of the moon. So before we move forward to the fun stuff, let's take a look at how moon magic came to be.

A Brief History of Moon Magic

Continuously seen as a source of abundance, the moon has been linked to wisdom, fertility, rebirth, and magic in various cultures throughout history. As our ancestors gazed up at the night sky, they would marvel at the nocturnal orb that would change shape each night in contrast to the extremely bright and consistently round sun. They eventually learned to use the moon's phases as a source for measuring time, tracking menstrual cycles, and forecasting the weather. They even came to celebrate the moon as a deity in all its glowing glory.

While the moon is mostly associated with femininity and modern goddess worship today, ancient cultures initially identified the moon as male. First recorded in 3500 BCE in Sumer and continuously worshipped well into 250 CE in Syria, the earliest and most significantly known moon god was Nanna, also known as Sin. Birthed in the underworld, he would rise from the horizon and stretch across the night sky, becoming a patron deity of Sumer and worshipped in the Ziggurat of Ur. In fact, the moon had such significance to the people that it held a higher status than the sun, which they considered to be Nanna's son, Utu. Nanna's moon cult even included the earliest known poet, Enheduanna, who acted as his high priestess, elevating him in her writings along with his daughter Inanna, the goddess of love and Queen of Heaven.

The Egyptians also worshipped lunar male deities in contrast to mostly female solar deities. Khonshu and Thoth were two specific gods who had governance of the moon and time. It was not until the Hellenic period in Greece that the moon became feminized with a variety of goddesses—especially Selene (called Luna by the Romans), who was the ultimate personification of the moon. The Greeks also had moon myths surrounding Artemis, the goddess of the hunt and crescent moon, and Hekate, a titan goddess of the heavens, earth, and underworld.

While some cultures worshipped the moon with reverence, others feared it and believed that it was the chief source of evil. With the rise of patriarchal monotheistic religions, cultures shifted away from those that celebrated the goddess and moon. One of the most notable examples was Lilith, whose origins come from Sumerian time as the possible mother of Nanna, priestess of Inanna; as the wind spirit, she was later adopted and demonized by the Hebrews as Adam's first wife. There are many ancient myths of Lilith in folklore and religions alike, all connecting her to the moon as an evil witch and lustful demon. In modern times she has been elevated as a source of empowerment and a celebrated moon goddess of witchcraft.

It is from the contributions of our ancestors that we revel in the beauty and bounty of the moon now. Today, the ancient practices of moon worship have been resurrected by neo-paganism and other contemporary spiritual movements as they attempt to revive polytheistic and nature-based practices of premodern Europe. Within many of these practices lies adoration for ritual magic and witchcraft, which draws upon the energy of the moon. Ritual ceremonies called Esbats are moon celebrations held by various groups or individuals identifying as witches, pagans, and Wiccans. In these practices, we often combine our intentions with lunar energy to create change in the form of spells. These practices have fused the ancient ways with modern times, reigniting fascination with the moon and its primordial power for manifestation and abundance. With all this in mind, let's explore just how the influence of the moon's phases can bring abundance into your life.

Astrology, Astronomy, and Moon Magic

Around 3000 BCE, the Babylonians were at the forefront of astronomical observation, tracking the movements of the moon and sun to measure time. By 2000 BCE, they had extended their observations to include the positions of the planets. Moreover, they began to distinguish several constellations that the moon and sun passed through. They called this the zodiac, creating the 12 astrological zodiac signs we know today. From this, the Babylonians started to interpret omens based on their celestial observations.

In astrology, it is commonly known that your sun sign is a representation of your persona in this lifetime. This is the sign we are most aware of, but there is also a moon sign, which governs your emotional body. Where your sun sign dictates your daily life on a basic scale, your moon sign represents your subconscious soul and inner feelings.

Your moon sign is determined by the position of the moon at your time and place of birth. You can go to astro.com to cast your entire natal horoscope for free. Some individuals may not have access to their birth time or location. While it is ideal to have this information, you can still utilize the website using "unknown" options to receive the best prediction possible.

Knowing your moon sign can ultimately enhance your moon magic. I've found that working spellcraft when the moon is in your corresponding sign strengthens the magic! For instance, my moon sign is in Libra, and I feel more invigorated, magical, and potent whenever the moon is in that zodiac placement. Because of this, I save my most special rituals and spells for the full moon in Libra.

Cycles and Phases of the Moon

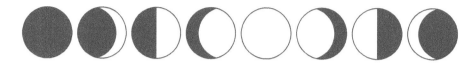

The moon's life cycle takes place over the course of 29.5 days. This known fact helped contribute to the invention of calendars in ancient times as people looked up at the continuously changing lunar orb in the night sky. The moon's cycle appears to grow and diminish in a clockwise motion as it reflects light from the sun down to earth. Because the moon is continuously ebbing and flowing in its orbital life cycle, it changes each night. However, the moon's phases have been divided into eight key times, each of which carries a different energetic imprint that can further assist in your magical efforts. Let's examine them in more detail.

NEW MOON

A new moon is the phase when no light reflects from the moon. Therefore, during this phase, the moon is not visible in the sky. This is because the moon is directly between the sun and Earth, preventing light from reflecting. This phase is all about creating an intention. Think of the new moon as a clean slate with endless opportunity. This is the birth of something new and a time to think about how you want to begin manifesting abundance in your life.

It is sometimes said that there are three days of the new moon. This is not necessarily true. The nights before and after the new moon also appear to be total blackness, at least from our perspective here on earth, as the crescent is too small to see with the naked eye. The night before the new moon is sometimes called the dark moon and is considered the most powerful time for banishing and introspection.

WAXING CRESCENT

 The waxing crescent resembles a backward "C" and is the first step on the moon's journey to reaching fullness. This phase is actually visible during the day and becomes more visible as the sun sets. When it comes to cultivating abundance, this phase is all about taking action.

FIRST QUARTER

 The first quarter is when the moon's illumination is at 50 percent, showing only on the right side of the moon's surface. Because the moon is in a half-full state, it can represent a crossroads, and this can be a potent time for casting abundance in regard to making decisions.

WAXING GIBBOUS

 The waxing gibbous phase is when the moon is almost all the way full but is missing a "C"-like edge on its left side. Moving from the previous phase of decision-making, it is here that your spellcrafting should get more specific as you home in on your intentions.

FULL MOON

 The full moon is the most glorified phase of the moon. It is a full climax of energy and has been a central focus of folklore and worship. It is common for witches and other members of the magical community to take this time to celebrate the glory of the moon and draw down lunar abundance into themselves. This phase is perfect for magical work that amplifies your intentions while also reflecting and magnifying beauty and grace.

Just like the new moon, it is commonly said that there are three days of the full moon. While the exact full moon phase lasts only a brief second, to our eyes here on Earth, it appears that the moon is full for a total of three days. If you want to utilize full moon energy but have a conflicting schedule on the actual night of it, you will still be able to utilize its energy the day before and the day after.

WANING GIBBOUS

The waning gibbous is the flip side of the waxing gibbous. Here, the moon will start to retract in size from its right side. In this phase, it is best to focus on gratitude as you express thanks for the abundance that has manifested in your life.

THIRD QUARTER MOON

Like the first quarter, the third quarter phase is when the moon's visibility is cut completely in half—only this time, it is the left side that is illuminated. As the moon appears to diminish further, the central theme of abundance here is forgiveness.

WANING CRESCENT

The waning crescent resembles a "C"-shaped sliver and will rise after midnight, remaining visible in the early morning hours. In this final stage of the moon before it rebirths into a new phase, it is a time to let go and release. Your witch work will be best focused on clearing the things in your life that hold you back.

Additional Moon Phenomena

In addition to the common eight phases of the moon, there are several other moon stages that provide an extra oomph of abundance to spellcasting.

Black Moon: A time when two new moons are featured within the same month. Not to be confused with the astrological black moon.

Blue Moon: A time when two full moons are featured within the same month.

Red Moon: The name given to the moon during a total lunar eclipse.

This phenomenon is the result of Earth moving directly between the sun and moon, giving the moon a red color. This phase is also sometimes referred to as a blood moon.

Solar Eclipse: When the moon moves directly between the sun and Earth, blocking the light of the sun.

Supermoon: When a new or full moon is at its closest position to Earth. These moons (when full) appear much bigger and brighter than other moons.

Natural Lunar Energy

Everything within the universe is composed of energy—physical, emotional, and spiritual. Magic and spellcraft manipulate this energy for manifestation. Working with the power of the moon's force can help empower your life and provide the energy necessary to manifest more of what you want! To better understand the metaphysical energy of the moon, it is good to get a more detailed sense of how it scientifically affects life on Earth.

We all know that the moon influences gravity and the tides of the ocean. During the new and full moons, Earth becomes positioned in a line between the sun and moon. The parts of the earth that are in this line experience high tides from the gravitational pull of the sun and reinforcement of the moon. Simultaneously, the parts of Earth that are at a 90-degree angle to the alignment of the sun and moon will experience low tides. While each moon phase affects plant growth, the gravitational pull of a full moon allows plants to absorb more water. Similarly, this also affects the water of our atmosphere, giving the moon power over weather. It has been observed that more hurricanes and tornadoes occur during the full and new moons, while more rainfall is experienced during the waxing and waning phases.

On the subject of water, roughly 70 percent of the earth is made up of it, and the human body is close to 60 percent. Science has confirmed that the moon has no effect on the human body, yet the closeness in water percentage of the earth and the human body can further illustrate the spiritual significance and energy link between humans and the moon.

The moon is also linked specifically to people with periods through menstruation. While it is not necessarily true that all periods sync to the lunar cycle, there is a scientific connection to each cycle's time line—29.5 days! Even the word "menstruation" derives from the Latin word "mensis," meaning "month," which comes from the Greek word "mene," which means "moon." Meanwhile, a variety of animals rely on the moon's cycles to live. Some use lunar light for hunting or hiding, while others use it for mating. Certain marine species and amphibians use the moon's full and/or new moon tides to come ashore to mate.

With this in mind, it is obvious that lunar energy has a direct effect on our lives. As we continue, we will further explore how we can transmute these characteristics into energy for manifestation and abundance with acts of witchery.

The Moon, Manifestation, and Abundance

It is a common misconception that the new and full moons are the most abundant phases for creating intention and manifestation. In reality, each phase of the moon can be used to set intentions, imagine success, inspire self-knowledge, build power, and help us let go of what is holding us back. These are essentially all forms of calling abundance into our lives. "How?" you may ask. Well, we've all heard that imitation is the highest form of flattery. This is similar to how and why moon magic works. Through a process known as sympathetic magic, we can manipulate energy based upon the laws of similarity.

The majority of magical practices are sympathetic in nature—essentially drawing upon the comparison of things to achieve transformation. Spells will commonly include a variety of materials, such as crystals, herbs, and incenses, to help further pack a punch of manifestation. For example, when it comes to spellcraft, red candles are a common accessory in love spells because red is associated with love and passion. Likewise, the use of figures like dolls or poppets can be used to represent yourself or another person in magical practices. In the next chapter we will get specific and hone in on how to utilize different ingredients to further cultivate your lunar abundance.

CHAPTER 2

Your Abundant Lunar Tool Kit

Think of your moon magic and spells like cooking your favorite dish. Before you can get started, you first must decide what kind of meal you are going to make. From there, you select a recipe based upon your desire. The recipe here is the spell, and it has a formula for execution. Just like cooking, your spellcasting recipes are going to have a variety of ingredients that are mixed together to achieve the desired result. However, instead of mixing culinary ingredients, we are mixing a variety of natural items that correspond with our desired goals. Instead of cooking them in an oven or on a stovetop, your spells are cast with the intention that you pour into them.

How, When, Why, and Where

In this section, we will review the correct methodology, impact of time, and importance of place when it comes to casting your moon spells. Please refer back to this section if in doubt while weaving your witchery in part 2.

MYSTICAL MOON METHODOLOGY: THE HOW

There are certain steps one must take before jumping into any spell or ritual. As we move forward through this chapter, keep the following outline in mind for executing your lunar witchcraft.

Moon Magic Preparation Outline

1. **Determine your intention.** This is the most important part! Have a clear understanding of what you desire and how you want it to manifest in your life.

2. **Gather your supplies.** In the end, the only supplies you must have are yourself and your will. However, we utilize additional tools to help amplify this energy for manifestation. We will touch on this more throughout the chapter.

3. **Arrange your space.** Your rituals, ceremonies, and spells will require the utmost focus. Therefore, it is very important to plan for potential distractions. This might include disruptive pets, family members, roommates, weather conditions, a ringing phone, and a slew of other possibilities. In preparation for the ritual, make sure that you have addressed these factors and thought about any other potential distractions that might come your way.

4. **Take a bath or shower.** I recommend bathing before a ritual to physically and energetically cleanse yourself in preparation for your conjuration. *Witch Tip:* A bath can be a spell all on its own, where you are an ingredient. But we'll touch on that more later.

Once all of the groundwork is complete, there comes the process of conducting your moon magic. The following is a simple, step-by-step outline for a standard ritual format. Each of these will be explored in further detail throughout the chapter.

Moon Magic Ritual Outline

1. **Purify the space.** This can be as simple as sprinkling pure salt water, using a sage stick, or sweeping the area in preparation for your ritual.

2. **Ground and center.** Once all is in place, it is time to ground and center. This is a meditative process that clears your mind and focuses your energy on the ritual ahead.

3. **Cast the circle.** This involves creating an energetic boundary between the realms to cultivate your mooncraft (see page 23).

4. **Call the quarters/elements.** This helps anchor the boundaries of your circle and also pulls in the energy of the elements to further assist in your magical rite (see page 22).

5. **Call the moon/deity.** This is for calling on a lunar deity, ancestors, or spirit for assistance in your great work. This is an optional practice.

6. **Declaration of intent.** This is where you perform your spell or celebration. *Fun fact*: We call them spells because this is where you "spell" out your intention through the power of word.

7. **Raising energy.** A practice of stirring up the energy and pushing it into the universe.

8. **Cakes and ale.** An act of gratitude in honor of the moon for its assistance.

9. **Ritual release.** Thank the moon, deities, elements, and universe for attending your ritual and for the blessings that are to come your way. Offer gratitude in preparation for the abundance you are to receive and close the circle.

TIMING IS EVERYTHING: THE WHEN

One mistake that many people make when starting on their moon magic journey is casting a bunch of spells at the same time. Remember: Moderation is key! This is because putting too much energy into the universe can cause a bit of confusion and adversely mix up the results. Therefore it is best to reserve spells for special occasions or needs. That said, aside from the moon's phases being an integral part of the timing of magic, the days of the week and months and the astrological signs also offer energy to draw upon.

Planetary Hours and Days of the Week

The planetary hours are considered a special astrological system where hours and days of the week are ruled by one of the seven classical planets: Saturn, Jupiter, Mars, the sun, Venus, Mercury, and the moon. Developed in ancient times, each day was given a planetary ruler and then divided into 24 hours that are associated with a specific planetary energy. You can utilize planetary energy in your mooncrafting to enhance your witchery. For instance, Venus is the planet of love and rules over Friday. A spell to attract new love into your life would be best performed during the new or waxing crescent moon phase, on a Friday, during the planetary hour of Venus.

But what happens if the moon phase doesn't land on the right day of the week? Use the planetary hour best associated with the energy you need. For example, if I wanted to do a money spell but could not do so on a Thursday, I would instead work it during the planetary hour most associated with finance (Jupiter) on the day that I could. I use astrology .com.tr/planetary-hours.asp to help me determine the planetary hour in accordance with my geographical location. See the following chart for more details.

DAY	PLANETARY RULER	PLANETARY SYMBOL	CORRESPONDING ENERGY
Monday	Moon	☽	Emotions, intuition, psychic awareness, and enchantment
Tuesday	Mars	♂	Passion, sexuality, competition, bravery, and aggression
Wednesday	Mercury	☿	Communication, education, new ideas, and health
Thursday	Jupiter	♃	Luck, growth, accomplishment, finances, and legal matters
Friday	Venus	♀	Love, beauty, indulgence, luxury, self-care, and pleasure
Saturday	Saturn	♄	Long-term goals, career, karma, and reversals/banishing
Sunday	Sun	☉	Empowerment, enthusiasm, energy, wealth, and success

Moon Months

Different civilizations have given monthly names to the moon, particularly full moons. This chart identifies some of the common Indigenous American full moon names and associated magical efforts that can be drawn upon for your moon spells.

MONTH	NAME	NAMED AFTER...	MAGICAL EFFORTS
January	Wolf Moon	Wolves howling in the cold	Family, friendship, leadership
February	Snow Moon	The month with the heaviest snowfall	Home activities
March	Worm Moon	Earthworms seen in the soil with the arrival of spring	Planting, goals, and health
April	Pink Moon	The pink spring flowers	Love and beauty
May	Flower Moon	The abundance of flowers in bloom	Creation and fertility
June	Strawberry Moon	Strawberry-picking season	Prosperity
July	Buck Moon	Deer growing their antlers	Strength and physical energy
August	Sturgeon Moon	The fish filling the Great Lakes	Communication
September	Harvest Moon	Crops ready for harvest	Gratitude
October	Hunter's Moon	Autumnal hunting rituals	Empowerment and primal instinct
November	Beaver Moon	Beavers preparing for winter	Preparation and protection
December	Cold Moon	The arrival of winter	Renewal and success

Zodiac Signs

Both astronomy and astrology utilize the zodiac, a series of
12 constellations that the sun, moon, and planets move through.
The moon transitions into a new zodiac sign every two to three days.
The zodiac provides certain energy types that can be utilized in your
spellcasting. Many almanacs will identify which sign of the zodiac
the moon is in, but I like to refer to mooncalendar.astro-seek.com when
planning my spells around the zodiac.

MOON SIGN	MAGICAL EFFORTS
Aries	Action, empowerment, rebirth
Taurus	Love, home, prosperity
Gemini	Communication, travel, intelligence
Cancer	Emotions, compassion, family
Leo	Attention, courage, power
Virgo	Intellect, job seeking, health
Libra	Justice, beauty, art
Scorpio	Secrets, sexuality, transformation
Sagittarius	Truth, luck, passion
Capricorn	Career, politics, ambition
Aquarius	Friendship, technology, freedom
Pisces	Spirituality, psychic power, intuition

ABUNDANCE FOR ALL OCCASIONS: THE WHY

Ritual and the art of ceremony help stimulate mental magic. We naturally perform various rituals every day—our morning routine, commute
to work, etc. The idea of performing rituals to manifest abundance is not
much different. Spiritual ceremonies and ritual magic ultimately help
shift your daily struggles into positivity.

I love the entire process of putting a ritual together. My mind immediately goes from the chaotic pressures of the mundane world into a
place of profound bliss. I also think that it is really important to have fun

with your magical work. Yes, these rituals are serious and require a great deal of focus, but they should provide you with joy and happiness while releasing what no longer serves and cultivating an enchanted life on your own terms.

SACRED SPACES AND PLACES: THE WHERE

One of the great things about our modern spiritual practices is that we are not limited when it comes to the spaces in which we conduct our ceremonies. Spells can be performed in a wide array of places, both inside and outside, as long as they are in a private setting. Magic is mental, fueled by intent. If you are in a place full of distractions, you run the risk of limiting your capacity for abundance.

It can be advantageous to cast your lunar magic in the great outdoors, but it is important to remember safety as well as permission. Certain outdoor locations are prohibited, while others make it easy for attack or injury to occur from natural causes. Also, the elements can be a bit challenging for outdoor spaces. I once hosted a group outdoor ritual, and no matter how hard we tried, the wind came raging in and extinguished our candles. Then there is always rain—it can be a real pain.

Because of this, I tend to prefer indoor settings and will set up a workspace in my living room. I recommend that you do so in a place where you can directly see the moon, but sometimes this is not possible due to your location, or even weather influences. If you are unable to see the moon, do not fret. The moon is always there, just like the stars and countries on the other side of the planet. We don't have to *see* it to know it is there or to harness its power. However, if you are a particularly visual person, you can certainly utilize a photograph, statue, or other symbolic reference to the moon phase you are using in your work.

Setting and Manifesting Intentions

Remember that you are not limited to manifesting abundance during only one moon phase. The process of materializing your manifestation comes from working your intention through an entire moon cycle. Between the new and full moons, set your intentions in new beginnings, action, decisions, and celebration. From full to new, focus on gratitude, forgiveness, and release.

When it comes to manifesting your intentions, remember my three simple Moon Magic Mantras:

- **Ask for what you want.** In order to get it, you have to be willing to ask for it and follow through. It is often said that magic is fueled by your intent. This is true, but you also must be willing to use your will.
- **Believe it will manifest.** Belief is powerful. In order to get what you've asked for, it is imperative that you suspend your skepticism and truly believe it will manifest. This is where the laws of attraction come in—believe it will happen and it will; believe it won't and it won't.
- **Receive abundance.** This is the best part! Once you open yourself up to the possibility of the abundance the moon can give you, you will become a magnet to draw more and more abundance into your life.

When manifesting your intentions, it is best *not* to be limited with your desires. By limiting your intention, you limit your abundance. This means that if you are looking to bring love into your life, it is best to focus solely on bringing that romantic and passionate love to you rather than on a specific person.

Results may be instantaneous, or they may take some time. The universe does not operate on our sense of time. Spellcasting is not a fast-food spiritual practice. Have patience and faith that things are working according to plan. Worst-case scenario: If your manifestation does not happen within a six-month time frame, try again. But remember, it is important to act both practically and magically. You have to *do* the work in the real world to achieve the benefits.

Meditation and Moon-Bathing

Meditation is an act of stilling the mind and can include focusing on a particular intention. It is a very rewarding act that can be used for a number of situations.

Moon-bathing is the art of absorbing lunar energy by allowing the moon's rays to illuminate your skin to the same extent of sunbathing.

Witch Tip: Place a container of fresh spring water with a tumbled moonstone inside of it on a windowsill during the night of a full moon. Be sure to collect it before sunrise and store in a dark place afterward. Apply the water to your skin to achieve the same effects of moon-bathing whenever you need a burst of full moon abundance.

The Recipe for Ritual

As with any recipe, there are ingredients and steps you must take to reach the desired outcome. The same is true for your lunar rituals, ceremonies, and spellcraft. In this next section we will take a look at the methodology associated with creating lunar rituals and the corresponding tools of spellcasting.

TOOLS OF THE TRADE

There are several tools that are traditionally used in modern witchcraft. These are used to assist in different stages of the ritual. The most common ones across the board are:

• **Athame:** An often magnetized double-edged blade that is used to direct energy. It is not used to cut anything physical. In rituals, it is an extension of you and is used to cast a circle, cut boundaries, enchant items, etc. Some traditions have further specifics, such as the length of the blade and the material of the handle. I say whatever has meaning to you only furthers your intention. Mine is a voluptuous mermaid cast in brass. As a mermaid, she helps me tap into lunar energies by way of water energy and the tides the moon controls. It is by far my most meaningful witch tool.

• **Wand:** Made of wood, metal, or even crystal, a wand is used to conjure and is often interchangeable with an athame.

• **Pentacle:** This is a wood, clay, or metal disc that contains the famous witch symbol of the five-pointed star. It is symbolic of the human experience and astronomy. In rituals it is used as a consecration tool.

• **Chalice:** A drinking vessel and offering cup used for lunar libations. It can be anything from a standard water glass to a bedazzled wineglass.

• **Cauldron:** An iron pot with three legs that generally holds fire or other items. Can be substituted with a fireproof bowl for burnings.

• **Mortar and pestle:** This is used to grind and blend incense and magical powders.

- **Tarot cards:** A set of 78 cards used to reflect and predict future outcomes. The cards use imagery and symbolism that stimulate the subconscious mind and provide signs for interpretation. Many witches and modern mystics incorporate tarot cards or other divination tools, such as oracle cards or crystal balls, into their practices.
- **Book of Shadows:** The infamous spell book! This is generally considered a witch's diary or journal, where they write down their spells, intentions, visions, and other important parts of their individual practice.

THE FOUR DIRECTIONS AND ELEMENTS

Each cardinal direction represents one of the four major elements—earth, air, fire, and water. Within many neo-pagan practices, nature is seen as sacred. In many ways the moon is a part of the natural world we live in. Within your circle formations, it is customary to call the quarters/elements into the space to provide further energy. When doing this, I prefer to start in the east, as the moon moves from east to west. Here is a look at the correspondences associated with each element:

- **East:** Associated with the element of air. Air has no physical appearance, and so it is representative of our mind, thought, intellect, and imagination. In rituals it can be represented by a feather, incense, or a bell.
- **South:** Associated with the element of fire, which is a representation of desire, sensuality, passion, and creativity. In rituals it can be represented by a candle, volcanic glass (obsidian), or desert sand.
- **West:** Associated with the element of water. It is connected to the emotional current within us and the love that pours out of us. In rituals it can be represented by seashells, dried starfish, or a bowl of water.
- **North:** Associated with the element of earth, which is symbolic of structure, organization, and material power. In rituals it can be represented by a crystal, rock, leaf, plant, or bowl of salt.

Witch Tip: I know . . . cardinal directions can be hard! But luckily there are apps on our smartphones that show us which direction is which.

However, if you are in doubt and do not have a compass on you, think about your position in relation to the sun, which rises in the east and sets in the west. At midday, it hangs in the south. The sun never sits in the northern position if you live in the northern hemisphere of Earth.

CASTING YOUR MOON CIRCLE

A common term used in spellcasting is "circle." Circles are utilized to contain the magic of a ritual and act as a slingshot for the magic conjured during it. A circle also provides protection between the realms of the astral plane and the mundane world. When I cast circles for the moon, I visualize them as an energetic sphere, mimicking the shape of the moon and our home—Earth.

There are contrasting opinions on how large a circle should be. However, our spaces are more limited now than ever and don't always provide for a six- or nine-foot circle. Don't get too hung up on these specifics. Be imaginative, and let your magic be an extension of you. As long as you are comfortable and able to fit what you need in the space, you are good.

It can be a powerful gesture to mark the boundaries of your circle with chalk, salt, ivy, flower petals, candles, or a representation of each corresponding element (such as incense for air, a candle for fire, a glass of water for water, and a flower or plant for earth).

Once you have selected your intent, gathered your supplies, cleansed yourself, and purified the area, simply cast the circle by holding your athame, wand, or other tool, such as a crystal or incense stick, and drawing the circle in a clockwise motion around your space.

Hold your athame or wand up to the sky and drag it down to the ground in front of you. Close your eyes and trace the circle around your space. As you do, visualize a silver lunar light being pulled down from the moon and sprayed outward, creating a glittery ring around you. As you do this, say:

I conjure thee, sacred circle of lunar power.

May you protect and promote the abundance conjured here within.

Now face the eastern side of your circle. Holding your air representation, call:

Guardians of the east, element of air, bless this circle with your inspiration.

Now face the southern side of your circle. Holding your fire representation, call:

Guardians of the south, element of fire, bless this circle with your passion.

Now face the western side of your circle. Holding your water representation, call:

Guardians of the west, element of water, bless this circle with your love.

Now face the northern side of your circle. Holding your earth representation, call:

Guardians of the north, element of earth, bless this circle with your structure.

Point your athame or wand above you and move the tip to the ground beneath you in a swift sweep, saying:

As above, so below.

Point your athame or wand to your left and swiftly move it to your right, saying:

As with, so without.

Visualize the circle expanding into a sphere around you while saying:

May this circle be blessed in lunar abundance.

Now your circle has been created. It is here that you state your intent. This can be as simple as a meditation to help further your goal, conducting a specific spell from part 2 based on your intention, or calling upon a specific moon deity or ancestors to assist with the work or to honor in reverence. For those choosing to work with a deity (see page 34 for a list of some lunar deities), you may use the following template if you do not otherwise have an invocation dedicated to them:

[God or goddess name], *god/dess of* [what they are known for],
I call upon you and ask that you extend your services to this
magical working.

Once your intent has been completed, the next part is raising the energy and creating a cone of power. This helps churn up the energy of your circle to slingshot it into the universe for manifestation. This can be done by dancing, chanting, ringing bells, using a sound bowl, etc.

After you've worked up physical energy, you may wish to make a toast to the moon with a lunar libation as an act of gratitude to the moon and grounding for yourself. After this you will begin to close your circle by thanking each element in a counterclockwise movement and relinquishing the circle. To do this, hold your athame or wand outstretched in front of you. Moving in a counterclockwise direction, visualize the circle being sliced in half as the silver sparkle disintegrates up to the moon while you say:

May my lunar circle be open with these words spoken.

Adornments, Enhancements, and Accoutrements

Now that we have explored some of the hows and whys, let's get more specific and drill down on the ingredients we can use in lunar witchcrafting.

FOOD AND BEVERAGE

It is best not to enter your spellcasting with a full stomach, as it can cause discomfort or present an adverse reaction that pulls you away from your moon manifestations. That said, food and beverage can be added to your workings to further enhance the energy, to ground, and to act as offerings in exchange for your desires.

If incorporating foods into your spellcasting, think about what the overall goal of the spell is and build from there. I won't always include food in my rituals, but when I do, I have found that succulent fruits, cookies, cakes, and other decadent snacks work best.

I do always include some kind of lunar libation in my rituals. For this, I prefer to use champagne or wine. Teas, tonics, and tinctures can also be great additions to your workings, as you can blend them in advance with herbs relevant to your manifestation goals.

CLOTHING

The fashion world has embraced witchcraft, and we see lots of long, flowing shawls, kimonos, and cosmic prints that enhance aesthetic allure. When it comes to your spellcasting attire, the choice is up to you for how to decorate yourself. Ideally, it should be something special that you reserve only for your witch work. It is best to wear something that is comfortable and allows for easy movability. I have several sequined kimonos and satin robes that I prefer to use in my ritual spaces to enhance the magic I conjure. However, it is important to make sure that your clothing does not interfere with your work. As gorgeous as a flowing fringed cape may be, it might not be practical when it comes to walking around a circle of flames.

Depending on the type of abundance you are trying to manifest, you may want to dress in the color associated with your goal (see page 29). Remember that everything is made up of energy and that colors are an additional energy source to draw upon.

Alternatively, you may choose to wear nothing at all. This practice is often called "skyclad," meaning clad only in the sky. This can be a potent type of work, especially for full moon rituals, to help absorb the light of the moon.

MUSIC

I love incorporating music into my spellcasting. My personal choice for music includes sensual songs or lush remixes that synchronize to the energy of my lunar atmosphere. I will also sometimes look at song lyrics to determine the overall theme. For example, if you are working on bringing in an abundance of love, a song that is about a breakup would not be the best choice. Make sure that you research your musical choices ahead of time and have listened to them all the way through to ensure there are no unexpected moments. Ambient, electronic, folk, soul, trance, and trip-hop are some genres I'd recommend when exploring musical magic. Some of my go-to witchy-sounding musicians are Björk, Tori Amos, Lana Del Rey, Stevie Nicks, Massive Attack, Sade, FKA Twigs, Tennis, Florence and the Machine, Esthero, and SZA.

It is worth noting that if you are a musician of any kind, the playing of instruments, singing, or chanting can have a powerful effect on your workings. This will help raise the energy in your circle and then expel it into the universe.

Magical Extras, Accessories, and Add-Ons

Jewelry: In addition to your clothing, jewelry is a powerful accessory for magical workings. You will see a lot of witches or others within the magical community wear a variety of pendants and/or rings made of certain crystals to bring protection, luck, or another energy source. Any jewelry that is special to you can be cleansed and empowered by the moon to aid in your magical efforts.

Sigils: These are magical symbols that are aligned with the spell-caster's intent. These can be icons, letters, or words that are usually carved into candles for candle magic or drawn on paper and charged on your moon altar.

Mica: Mica flakes are a natural glitter alternative that can be added to your candles and other magical workings. You can dress your candles with different mica colors to imbue them with additional energy. Since mica naturally sparkles and reflects light, it is also a great agent to help draw in energy while protecting your intentions.

CANDLES

Candles come in a variety of shapes and colors that can help fuel intentions. Because candles are made of wax, many spellcasters will carve words or symbols into them, anoint them with oils and ground herbs, or add mica and other ingredients as they correspond to their desire. A good rule of thumb is that the candle must burn down completely for the spell to take place. Therefore, it is important to choose a candle size that works accordingly. For larger candles, it is more than okay to light the candle on multiple days while you meditate and focus on your desire. Just never use the same candle for multiple spells. If you are extinguishing the flame, I recommend blowing it out rather than snuffing it so that your breath, your life force, pushes the smoke into the universe for manifestation.

Here is a list of the various color associations that can be applied to candles, clothing, and any other element of ritual practice:

- **Red:** Power, passion, lust
- **Pink:** Beauty, harmony, love
- **Orange:** Confidence, vitality, creativity
- **Yellow:** Imagination, happiness, concentration
- **Green:** Health, earth power, prosperity
- **Blue:** Calm, peace, communication
- **Purple:** Vision, wisdom, spirituality
- **Brown:** Grounding, home, material
- **Gray:** Balance, legal work, invisibility
- **Black:** Protection, banishing, absorption
- **White:** Reflection, deflection, purity
- **Gold:** Success, luck, prosperity
- **Silver:** Intuition, victory, glamour
- **Rose gold:** Attraction, grace, flirtation

INCENSE AND FRAGRANCES

The burning of sacred herbs can act as an offering to supreme higher powers or ancestors, and the fragrance can alter your state of mind and encourage a trance experience. Incense can be purchased at local metaphysical stores and online. Online stores are a great resource for those in remote locations or who do not have spirituality stores near them.

- **Amber:** A wonderful mixture of resins and musks, amber is great for attracting luck and initiating new projects and goals.
- **Copal:** A spiritual resin and one of the most popular ingredients for spiritual cleansing.
- **Dragon's blood:** A favorite of mine. Dragon's blood is universal—it's a great incense to dispel negativity while promoting attraction of desires. Good for protection, courage, power, love, and strengthening intent.
- **Frankincense:** Commonly used to consecrate items and attract luck.
- **Gardenia:** A fragrant floral scent that attracts happiness, love, and peace.
- **Jasmine:** A calming floral that attracts love, money, and psychic vision.
- **Musk:** A very aphrodisiacal blend that is perfect for magic involving sensuality and self-care.
- **Nag champa:** An Indian blend that is one of the most popular incenses in the world. This is great for meditative works and spiritual awareness.
- **Patchouli:** Promotes attraction, especially when it comes to money, fertility, love, and lust.
- **Rose:** Another universal incense/fragrance that will stimulate love, peace, and spirituality.
- **Sandalwood:** A popular blend that is great for protection, psychic vision, and overall success.
- **Sage:** The most popular herb burned for protection and spiritual cleansings. Commonly used in home blessings.

CRYSTALS AND GEMSTONES

You can utilize the different moon phases to cleanse, charge, and empower your crystals. I like to hold the crystal to my heart, ask that it be empowered, and leave it to sit on a windowsill to absorb the energy of the night sky above.

Crystals harness an abundance of earth energy and are routinely used in energetic cleansings, feng shui practices, and metaphysics.

Be mindful when you are purchasing crystals, and make sure that they come from reputable sources that can identify the mines where they are from. There are a lot of fake crystals being sold on the market today that are plastic or glass. Likewise, anything that carries a fruit-type name like "raspberry" or "pineapple" quartz is likely color-treated. Some of the most common and easily found crystals today are:

• **Amethyst:** Easily classified as the modern mystic's favorite crystal. This deep purple crystal increases psychic awareness, mental clarity, and peace of mind.
• **Clear quartz:** The ultimate amplifier. Clear quartz can be utilized for all acts of magic.
• **Citrine:** Confidence, energy, and personal power.
• **Fluorite:** Comes in a variety of colors and in general represents clarity of mind and speech. It is a great stone to use for communication and is perfect for the office-bound #BossWitch.
• **Garnet:** Passion, strength, courage, and self-worth.
• **Labradorite:** This dark stone possesses a light-reflecting illusion that allows it to change color. Labradorite is a powerful stone of transformation, all acts of magic, and spirituality.
• **Moonstone:** The number-one crystal to use for moon magic. An exquisite stone to use for intuition, manifestation, and growth. Moonstone can be used as a physical representation of the moon in your rituals, especially when obtained as a sphere.
• **Obsidian:** A black volcanic glass that harmonizes negativity and clears mental blockages.

- **Pearl:** While not necessarily a crystal or gemstone, it is an important stone for moon magic, as it is created from mollusks that live in the water. Its nacre, or lustrous shine, resembles a full moon in all its glory. Pearls are stones of beauty, grace, and long-lasting love.
- **Pyrite:** Also known as fool's gold, pyrite is a golden, shiny crystal that sparkles with pure magic. It is a must-have stone for any magical worker as it reflects negativity and pushes it back to its sender.
- **Rhodonite:** This pink and black stone is a wonderful addition to moon rituals in the waning phase. It helps absorb depression and reintegrate it with imagination and harmony.
- **Rose quartz:** A common pink stone used for emotional healing, love, self-care, and fertility.
- **Selenite:** A very soft stone that gives off a lunar shine. It is great to use as a representation of the moon and promotes intuition, peace, and cleansing. *Witch Tip:* Do not soak selenite in water, or it will dissolve.
- **Smoky quartz:** A darker brown, gray, or black variation of quartz used for grounding, protection, and stirring up physical energy.
- **Tiger's eye:** Represents strength, courage, and catlike stealth.
- **Turquoise:** Perfect for spells that promote friendship, optimism, and emotional healing.

PLANTS, HERBS, AND ESSENTIAL OILS

In witchcraft, plants are used in their fresh or dried form to create potions, oils, and powders that align with your magical intent. They are also used in essential oils, both for topical treatment and for anointing ritual items such as candles. There is a great debate in witchland regarding the use of essential versus synthetic oils. My rule of thumb is essential is for topical healing while synthetic is for perfumes and allure. Here is a look at some of my favorite and most readily available plants used for potions, oils, and powders.

- **Basil:** Can be used for spells involving prosperity and protection.
- **Bay:** Bay leaves are perfect for good fortune and health.

- **Black pepper:** This spice is best used for magics that need a quick reaction, much like cinnamon. It is commonly used in spells for lust and protection or banishment.
- **Chamomile:** Chamomile promotes tranquility and does great in spells to cultivate compassion and heal fatigue.
- **Cinnamon:** One of my favorites! Cinnamon is a very spiritual spice that can be used in any working to speed up results—especially when it comes to anything that is sensual.
- **Elderflower:** A powerful defense flower for protection.
- **Hibiscus:** A fragrant and delicious floral. A powerful plant for attracting love and lust.
- **High John:** The root from a plant called *Ipomoea purga* or jalap; cousin to the morning glory and sweet potato. This is an incredibly powerful ingredient for many types of magic, including confidence, luck, strength, and overcoming obstacles.
- **Lavender:** A fabulously witchy herb that attracts harmony and peace.
- **Lemon:** This sweet and sour citrus is a common household fruit that helps attract love and good vibes while protecting against negativity and cleansing blockages.
- **Mint:** A good herb for prosperity and energy.
- **Mugwort:** Enhances intuition and induces prophetic dreams.
- **Neroli:** Stimulates feelings of happiness and confidence.
- **Orchid:** These work great in the bathroom, as moisture from your shower will keep them hearty. Place them in the reflection of a mirror to reflect beauty back to you.
- **Rose:** The queen of all flowers and a representation of love, beauty, health, luck, protection, and spirituality. Rose essential oil is one of the most expensive, coming in at roughly $100 for 10ml. A really great workaround is to find an inexpensive rose fragrance oil and add rose petals to it to bind the synthetic with the natural.
- **Rosemary:** An herb that is used for consecration of all types.
- **Tonka bean:** Perfect in spells associated with confidence and success.

- **Vanilla bean:** These are available from grocery stores and are a great ingredient for mental focus, love, and general attraction (physical and material).
- **Ylang-ylang:** Promotes sensuality and attention.

LUNAR DEITIES

Just as the moon is an energy source, deities are also a source of energy to draw upon. The following is a small list of some of the most influential deities associated with the moon. If any of them interest you, I recommend researching them a bit more and building a relationship with them before jumping right into asking them for help. In part 2, I will provide recommendations for which deities are best to integrate into your spells.

- **Aphrodite/Venus:** Greek/Roman goddess of love, beauty, and fertility. She was born from the sea and can be a very influential deity for lunar love magic.
- **Artemis/Diana:** Greek/Roman maiden goddess of the moon and the hunt. Patron goddess of feminist witches.
- **Hekate:** Greek goddess of witchcraft and magic. She is seen as a triple goddess and titan who governs the crossroads and the realms of the earth, moon, and underworld.
- **Khonshu:** Egyptian god of the moon whose name means "traveler," for he was seen traveling across the night sky.
- **Lilith:** Originally a Sumerian spirit linked to air, dreams, night, and seduction. She was later adopted by the Hebrews as Adam's first wife, who refused to submit to him. In modern times, she has been elevated to a goddess of witchcraft with many connections to the moon, independence, and equality.
- **Nanna/Sin:** Sumerian god, and one of the few male deities associated with lunar energy. His sacred animal was the bull, which was also linked to fertility.
- **Selene/Luna:** Greek/Roman titan goddess of the moon, known for driving a silver moon chariot across the sky at night. She is mostly associated with the full moon, intuition, and lunar psychic power.

- **Triple Goddess:** Seen in a variety of neo-pagan spiritualties, including the religion of Wicca, the Triple Goddess is a threefold representation of maiden, mother, and crone symbolizing the feminine life cycle with the waxing, full, and waning moon.
- **Yemaya:** An Afro-Caribbean mermaid goddess of the ocean, love, and healing often linked to witchcraft practices and the moon.

ALTARS

Altars are extremely personal and, as a result, should reflect the beauty and abundance you are trying to exemplify within your life. They are essentially your magical workstation and the focal point for the magic you conjure in your rituals. I feel it is best to be intuitive and place the items that are special to your desire wherever you feel is best.

In the most general of senses, your moon altar should house all of your ritual tools and have a representation of each element as previously discussed on page 22. Additionally, a lunar component should be included. This can be a statue of the moon, a photo, a silver pillar candle, a chunk of moonstone, or even a bouquet of white roses. You will apply the remaining supplies for your specific spellcasting as needed.

Now that we understand the whys and the hows of moon magic, let's explore the lunar abundance of each moon phase and how to set your intentions and look at several spells that can be performed for each.

Phases of the Moon

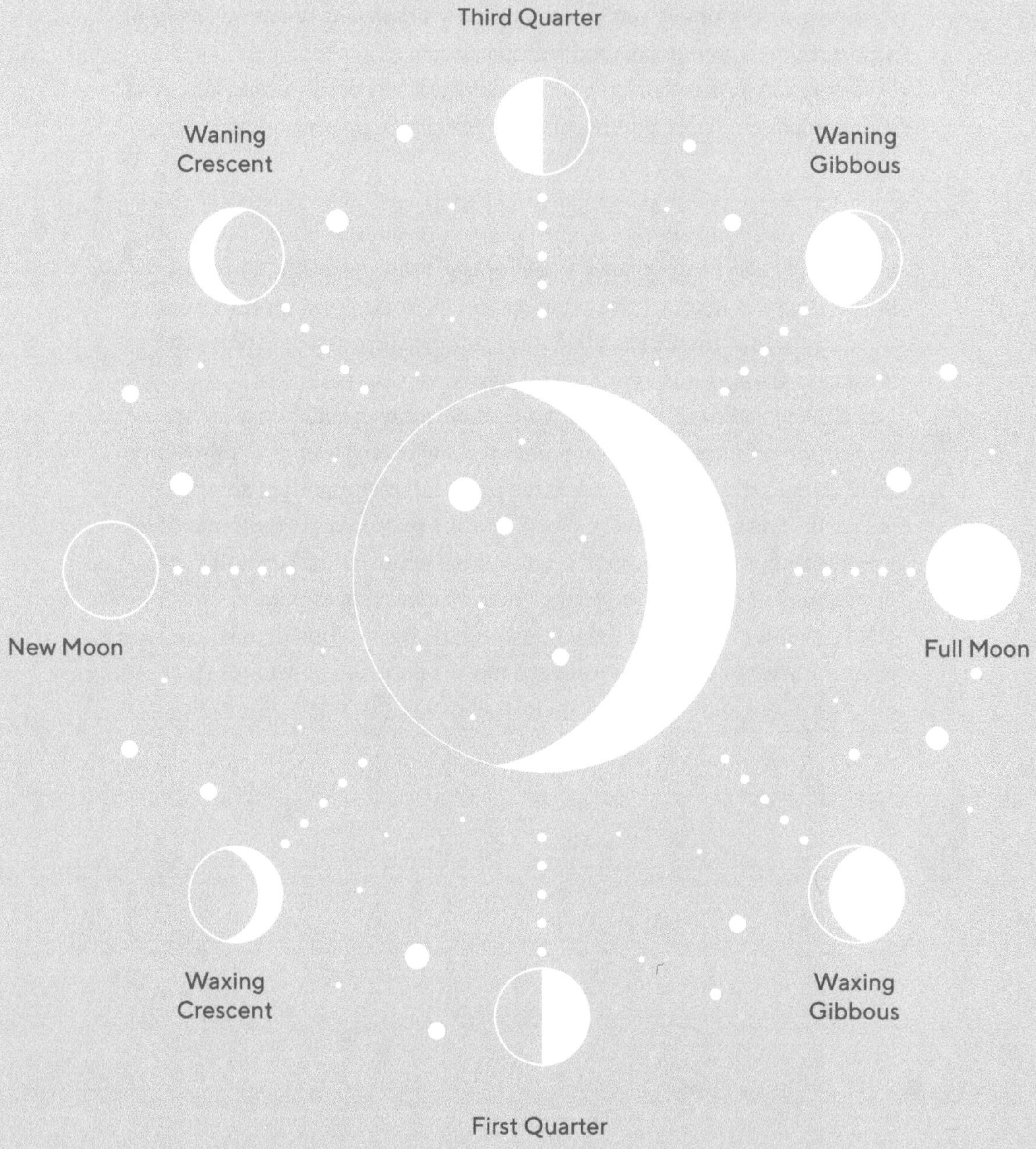

Third Quarter

Waning
Crescent

Waning
Gibbous

New Moon

Full Moon

Waxing
Crescent

Waxing
Gibbous

First Quarter

MOON SPELLS FOR ABUNDANCE

Welcome to part 2 of *The Complete Book of Moon Spells.* In the following chapters, we will use the material from earlier in the book to manifest our intentions through observation, meditation, and manifestation. Each chapter is devoted to one of the moon's eight phases and includes one herbal potion and eight spells corresponding to the associated phase. These spells and potions are centered around creating an abundance of love, success, joy, and peace. Each spell contains an easy-to-follow guideline for practice, as well as several optional considerations that you can build on if you see fit. Let's get started!

CHAPTER 3

New Moon:
Set Intentions

The new moon is a very potent conduit for manifestation. Remember that during this phase no visible light from the moon can be seen on earth. Much like when a seed has been planted underground, this is a time to focus on renewing goals, reconnecting to feelings, and setting desires aflame with new intentions. The following spells, ceremonies, and rituals are all connected with setting intentions for something new within your life.

Setting Your Intentions

Setting your intentions is the most important aspect of your moon magic. It doesn't always have to be as elaborate as a full-blown ritual or spell. It can be as simple as writing down your intentions, saying your affirmations, and meditating on your goals at your altar while observing the current phase lunar cycle. Your intentions can be anything you want them to be.

Use the following blank lines to write affirmations that align with your intentions for the new moon. These should all start with "I will," "I am," or "I have" rather than "I want" or "I need." This is because in order to manifest your reality, you must speak as though it already exists. Some examples are "I am healthy," "I am loved," and "I will find my love." Dream BIG and go for your goal!

_____

_____

_____

_____

_____

As the chapter continues, you will find a potion and eight spells that build on the intentions you'll set at the new moon. Each of these will include an affirmation that you should speak and visualize to draw abundance into your life.

Black Sky Potion

This new moon potion is a tea that can be brewed and incorporated into any new moon spell or ceremony, or any other magical effort to set intentions for new moon abundance. This potion is essentially a black tea blend, aiming to align with the blackness of the new moon. The cacao nibs add a chocolate flavor for sweetness while the orange zest helps stimulate the growth of new intention.

YOU WILL NEED (FOR A SINGLE SERVING):

1 teaspoon black tea leaves

½ teaspoon cacao nibs

½ teaspoon dried orange peel

Small mixing bowl

Hot water for brewing

FURTHER CONSIDERATIONS:

- **This is best mixed and brewed on any day during the planetary hour of the moon.**

- **Drink warm to stimulate the energy necessary for new growth and abundance.**

- **Make a larger batch and store the mixture in an airtight jar in a cool, dark space.**

PREPARING THE POTION:

1. Mix the tea leaves, cacao nibs, and dried orange peel together in a small mixing bowl with your hands. As you mix them, think about the affirmations you wrote down earlier on page 39 and ask that the herbs assist in bringing your intentions to fruition.

2. When ready to drink, place the blend in the hot water to brew. Let it steep for 5 minutes, give or take depending on your preferred flavoring of tea, and strain.

3. Sip on your potion slowly during any meditations you do during this time, or incorporate them into the spells that follow.

Attracting a Lover

Love spells can get tricky, because more often than not, people are looking to have a specific individual fall in love with them. However, this type of one-sided manipulation is ultimately not going to provide you with abundance. Therefore, it is better to cast a "come to me" love spell, which essentially lets the universe know that you are ready to attract a partner with the qualities you are looking for.

YOU WILL NEED:

Fresh red rose petals

2 drops rose oil, divided

2 drops ylang-ylang oil, divided

2 drops vanilla oil, divided

2 drops honey, divided

Mortar and pestle

Dried rose petals

Dried hibiscus petals

Paper

Red pen

Knife or toothpick

2 red candles to represent you and your soon-to-be lover

Fireproof plate or bowl

Rose quartz crystal

FURTHER CONSIDERATIONS:

- **Timing:** When the new moon falls on a Tuesday, Friday, or Sunday; in the planetary hour of Venus; or when the moon is in Taurus or Libra.

- **Attire:** Pink or red.

- **Incense:** Rose.

- **Deity:** Aphrodite/Venus, Selene/Luna, or Yemaya.

- **Affirmation:** "I will manifest my ideal love."

1. Prior to your spell, have a sensual ritual bath to invoke the elements of love. Add a handful of fresh red rose petals to your water with one drop of each oil (rose, ylang-ylang, and vanilla) and a drop of honey. As you bathe, envision yourself becoming a love magnet. Once finished, dry off and set up your ritual space with all the ingredients.

2. Use a mortar and pestle to grind your dried rose and hibiscus petals into a fine powder. While you do this, tell the herbs that they are going to help draw love to you. As you grind the petals, envision the love you want coming to you.

3. Now take your paper and pen and write a letter to the universe, moon, or spirit guides stating the qualities you are looking for in a mate.

4. Carve your name into the candle that represents you. Lick your finger and seal the carving with your saliva to lock your energy into the wax. Anoint both candles with one drop of each oil (rose, ylang-ylang, and vanilla) and honey. Top off the candles by evenly applying the rose and hibiscus powder to the candles.

5. Place your letter on the plate with the candles facing each other. In the center, place the rose quartz. Light the candles and say:

Come to me, I call you here.
I summon thee, a love that is true to me.
To possess the traits I long for,
And provide commitment, abundance, and more.

6. Now read your letter aloud. Focus on all the qualities you long for being imbedded into the person of your dreams. Once finished, blow the candles out, sending the smoke into the universe. Relight the candles each day during the planetary hour of Venus and visualize a lover coming to you.

Authenticity Spell

Sometimes society can project itself on you in such a harsh way that you are unable to be who you truly are. The following spell helps you remain true to yourself and be the most authentic version of yourself.

YOU WILL NEED:

Potted orchid flower

Framed photo of yourself

White candle

4 quartz crystals

Mirror

FURTHER CONSIDERATIONS:

- **Timing:** When the new moon falls on a Wednesday, Friday, Saturday, or Sunday; in the planetary hour of Mercury; or when the moon is in Aries, Leo, Libra, or Aquarius.

- **Attire:** Your favorite outfit.

- **Incense:** Your favorite.

- **Deity:** Lilith or Yemaya.

- **Affirmation:** "I am true to myself."

1. Place the orchid in the center of your altar with the framed photo in front of it and the white candle in front of the photo. Position the crystals around the candle.

2. Cradling one of the flowers, state:

> Orchid—*exotic flower that is unique,*
> *Help my authentic self to speak,*
> *To ebb and flow from this moment on.*

3. Light the candle and state:

> *In the darkest of nights, I shine bright.*
> *I call upon the true me to rebound, bloom, and be set free.*

4. Once the candle is burned out, place the crystals in the orchid pot. Store the orchid in a location that can be seen from a mirror. Every time you look at yourself, call upon the orchid to help your authenticity bloom.

Fertility Spell

This is a spell to stimulate fertility; however, it can be used by individuals who are looking to adopt a child as well.

YOU WILL NEED:

1 drop ylang-ylang oil
Green candle
Eco-friendly mica

Tumbled moonstone
A garden tree or potted indoor plant

FURTHER CONSIDERATIONS:

- **Timing:** When the new moon falls on a Monday, Friday, or Saturday; in the planetary hour of the moon, Venus, or Saturn; or when the moon is in Taurus, Cancer, or Capricorn.

- **Attire:** Pink or green.

- **Incense:** Rose, jasmine, or lavender.

- **Deity:** Aphrodite/Venus or Nanna/Sin.

- **Affirmation:** "I am fertile."

PERFORMING THE SPELL:

1. Place a drop of ylang-ylang oil on the candle. Sprinkle the mica on it. Light the wick, place the moonstone at the base of the candle, and say:

    By the power of the moon, I summon fertility in me.

2. Sit and envision pregnancy, the birth, the face of your future child—anything that further exemplifies your desire for parenthood. Extinguish the flame. Relight and meditate daily until the candle is completely spent.

3. Take any wax remains and the moonstone outside to a tree in your yard or to a potted indoor plant. Dig a hole where you will place the wax. Holding your moonstone, say:

> *Crystal of earth, named after the moon,*
> *Send me a baby sometime soon.*

Bury the crystal and wax remains. Continue to care for the tree or potted plant, and as you do, envision the family of your desire growing into fruition.

Job-Seeking Spell

Here is one of my favorite spells for finding a new job.

YOU WILL NEED:

Your résumé

Cauldron or fireproof bowl

1 green or gold taper candlestick

Toothpick

Lemon oil

FURTHER CONSIDERATIONS:

- **Timing:** When the new moon falls on a Thursday or Saturday; in the planetary hour of Jupiter or Saturn; or when the moon is in Sagittarius or Capricorn.

- **Attire:** Green or gold.

- **Incense:** Sandalwood.

- **Deity:** Nanna/Sin or Yemaya.

- **Affirmation:** "I have the best job."

PERFORMING THE SPELL:

1. Gently fold your résumé, set it aflame, and toss it into the cauldron, saying:

> *May the power of fire ignite the desire for finding the perfect job.*
> *May my qualifications be carried into the universe with the power of air.*

2. Carve your name into the wax of the candle on one side with the toothpick. Carve "career" on the other side.

3. Lick your thumb and trace it over the carving of your name to seal it with your biology. Anoint the candle with the lemon oil and roll into the ash of your résumé. Light the candle and focus on your intentions to find a new job. Focus on being called for an interview. Visualize yourself in the job you want. Lighting the wick of the candle, recite:

> With the lighting of this flame,
> I attract a career with worthful gain.

4. Let the candle burn all the way out. Submit your résumé to any and all jobs that catch your eye, knowing that the perfect fit will find you soon.

More Adventurous Spell

In my adolescence and early 20s, I was a very shy and timid person. I was always afraid to make the first move, answer first, or try something outside of my comfort zone. Being more adventurous allows you to experience more in the world. In this next spell you will create a mojo bag to carry on your person and attract adventure and ambition.

YOU WILL NEED:

Tiger's eye crystal

Dried mint

1 bay leaf

Orange cloth bag

Cinnamon oil

FURTHER CONSIDERATIONS:

- **Timing:** When the new moon falls on a Tuesday or Sunday; in the planetary hour of Mars or the sun; or when the moon is in Aries or Leo.

- **Attire:** Red, orange, or gold.

- **Incense:** Sandalwood.

- **Deity:** Artemis/Diana.

- **Affirmation:** "I am courageous. I am adventurous. I step outside of my comfort zone."

1. Arrange all of the ingredients in front of you on your moon altar. Tell each piece that you wish for it to aid in your magical working and help stimulate courage and a sense of adventure in you.

2. Add the crystal, mint, and bay leaf to the bag. Hold the opening to your mouth. Visualize your most adventurous, ambitious self and blow a deep but slow breath into the bag, giving life to your intention.

3. Tie the bag shut and anoint it with the oil. Carry the bag with you and anoint it once a week to feed it, reenergizing it with adventure.

New Moon Divination Ritual

Part of setting your intentions is making sure you are heading in the right direction. Witches will often use divination to discern what is coming next. Here we will call upon the darkness of the new moon to create a scrying vessel of black water. Scrying is a divination technique that involves gazing into an object to receive divine guidance on a situation. The guidance generally comes in thought form or flashes of images while you are in a trance state.

YOU WILL NEED:

2 black candlesticks

Bowl of water

Bouquet of white
roses (optional)

Black india ink

Tumbled black moonstone

FURTHER CONSIDERATIONS:

- **Timing:** When the new moon falls on a Monday; in the planetary hour of the moon; or when the moon is in Cancer, Scorpio, or Pisces.

- **Attire:** Black.

- **Incense:** Sandalwood.

- **Deity:** Hekate or Lilith.

- **Affirmation:** "In the darkness of night, I see my future with clarity and vibrancy."

1. Set up your altar so that your two black candlesticks are on the left and right sides of your bowl of water. Position the vase of roses, if you have one, behind the bowl of water. Have the india ink nearby.

2. Create a sacred space by conjuring your circle as detailed in chapter 2 (see page 23).

3. Once your circle has been cast, ground and center yourself into a meditative state. When ready, add five drops of black ink to the bowl of water. Say:

> *On this night of darkness, night of rebirth,*
> *I ask that this ink and water help me in my working*
> *and show me that which I need to see.*

4. Hold your black moonstone to the sky and say:

> *Crystal of the new moon, aid me in my working,*
> *And help show me that which I need to see.*

5. Place the crystal into the bowl of black water. Call upon your spirit guides, your higher power, or a god/goddess of the moon who is linked to occult wisdom, such as Lilith or Hekate, to assist in guiding you through the darkness. Speak to them from your heart or use any invocation that you may have created for this purpose.

6. Gaze into the water. Think about the intentions you want to manifest in your life at this moon phase. Allow yourself to drift in and out of consciousness, and make note of any ideas, thoughts, or visions that come to your mind.

7. Once the ritual is complete, take your bowl of water outside with one of the roses. Pour the water on the ground (india ink is nontoxic and environmentally safe). Place the rose on top of the wet ground as an offering to any spirit guides or deities that you called in for assistance with the ritual. Move forward on your journey, making note of any signs or messages that came to you during the ritual.

Relocation Spell

Sometimes we feel like we don't belong where we are. Other times we know that we have outgrown our current location and need to find a more suitable place to live. Whether you are looking for a new apartment, trying to buy a home, or even seeking to move to an unknown city, state, or country, this is a spell that will surely get you moving on to where you feel called to.

YOU WILL NEED:

Marker

Map that shows where you are and your desired destination (if unknown, use a world map)

Magnet

Pyrite crystal

Yellow candlestick with holder

Tonka oil

Gold eco-friendly mica

FURTHER CONSIDERATIONS:

- **Timing:** When the new moon falls on a Wednesday, Thursday, or Saturday; the planetary hour of Mercury, Jupiter, or Saturn; or when the moon is in Gemini or Sagittarius.

- **Attire:** Yellow, gold, or brown.

- **Incense:** Amber or frankincense.

- **Deity:** Artemis/Diana, Nanna/Sin, or Khonshu.

- **Affirmation:** "I will reside where I belong."

1. Gather all of your ingredients and set up your moon altar for ritual as described in chapter 2 (see page 35).

2. Using a marker, mark your current location on the map with a minus symbol. Mark your desired location on the map with a plus sign. These symbols will help illustrate positive and negative associations to your desired location. If your desired location is unknown, skip putting the plus sign on the map.

3. Clap your hands hard and rub them together vigorously to create static energy. When doing this, visualize energy drawing in and being pulled toward your hands from the moon. Now place the magnet in the center of your palms while in a prayer position. Enchant the magnet by saying:

> *Magnet, pull me to my new home.*
> *I ask that my new path be shown.*
> *Direct me near or far,*
> *Guiding me like the northern star.*

4. Place the magnet on top of the plus sign and place the pyrite on top of that. If your desired location is unknown, place the magnet and pyrite off the map, on the north side. Place the candle holder with the yellow candlestick directly behind the magnet and crystal from the perspective of your current location. Anoint the candle with tonka oil and sprinkle with the gold mica. When ready, light the candle and say:

> *Sacred flame on this dark night,*
> *Be the torch that gives my intention sight.*
> *Move me to the place I'm meant to be,*
> *For the good of all but mostly me,*
> *It is with my will that this will be.*

5. Let the candle burn out. Keep the map on your altar with the magnet in place. Regularly sit and meditate on your goal to relocate.

Calling Forth Your Animal Spirit

Some witches have what is known as a familiar—an animal spirit, living or passed, that is not only bound to the witch but also assists in their magical workings. These creatures are more than a pet—they are a magical partner.

YOU WILL NEED:

Photo of the animal you are drawn to (optional)

White candle in a jar

4 amethyst points

Sandalwood oil

FURTHER CONSIDERATIONS:

- **Timing:** This spell can be performed at any time regardless of the phase, day of the week, planetary hour, or what sign of the zodiac the moon is in.

- **Attire:** Animal print that connects to the animal spirit you desire (e.g., snakeskin print for snakes, cat prints for cats, faux furs, etc.). Alternatively, perform the spell skyclad.

- **Incense:** Nag champa.

- **Deity:** Any.

- **Affirmation:** "My animal spirit is bound to me."

1. If you are already drawn to a particular animal, select a photo of it and place it underneath a white candle in a jar.

2. Anchor the candle by placing the four amethyst point crystals (with their points facing in toward the candle) around the candle in the positions of the cardinal directions. Anoint the candle with the oil, light it, and say:

> *New moon of abundance, I ask of thee,*
> *To bring forth an animal spirit to me.*
> *May this spirit be found*
> *So that we may work in a pair and be bound.*

3. Visualize that your guide is coming to you, and repeat the visualizations with the candle lit daily until your magical pet is found.

CHAPTER 4

Waxing Crescent Moon: *Take Action*

As the moon turns to waxing crescent, this is a time to focus on taking action toward your goals and intentions. This is a time when the moon begins to ascend, so we must take heed and charge on ahead! If you planted seeds for abundance with the new moon, then you should continue tending to them with your meditations, affirmations, and visualizations. Just remember to be practical, too, and follow up on your intentions in the real world. If you didn't harness the power of setting intentions in the new moon phase, don't fret; just dive right in with action and determination.

POTION

SPELLS/RITUALS/CEREMONIES

Taking Action

Whether you are casting spells from this chapter, creating your own, or simply reflecting on the power of this moon phase with daily affirmations and meditations, it is important that you charge ahead and focus on actions that bring your goals closer to you. Take a moment now to write down and reflect on the actions you are taking to manifest your desires. These all come down to the art of doing. Some examples could be "I have applied for the job," "I have joined the dating app," and "I am making time for myself."

_____

_____

_____

_____

As the chapter continues, you will find a potion and eight spells that support the idea of taking action toward your intentions. Each of these will include an affirmation that should be spoken and visualized to draw abundance into your life.

Crescent Chai Potion

This potion is my take on a homemade chai tea. Known for its spicy and sweet flavors, the combination of ingredients helps stimulate activity and is perfect for your intentions associated with taking action. The recipe will make a batch that usually yields around six servings, and there are about six days of the waxing crescent. Therefore, store the leftovers in the fridge and enjoy a cup for each night of the phase.

YOU WILL NEED:

2 cinnamon sticks

6 cardamom pods

10 whole cloves

1 teaspoon black peppercorns

Mortar and pestle

1 teaspoon freshly grated ginger

6 cups water

1 cup black tea leaves

1 whole vanilla bean

FURTHER CONSIDERATIONS:

- This is best mixed and brewed on any day during the planetary hour of the moon.

- Drink warm to stimulate the energy necessary for action.

PREPARING THE POTION:

1. Place the cinnamon, cardamom, cloves, and peppercorns into a mortar and use the pestle to lightly crack to expose their flavor. Transfer the mixture into a saucepan with the ginger and water. Simmer on low heat for 10 minutes.

2. Add the black tea to the water and remove from the heat.

3. Cut the vanilla bean down its side and peel it open to expose a fragrant black powder inside. Scrape this into the pan and stir. Let the potion brew for 5 minutes, stirring occasionally in a clockwise motion, visualizing your intentions and how you plan to take action.

4. Strain the liquid and enjoy in any of your moon meditations, visualizations, or spellcasting for the waxing crescent.

Boost Confidence Bath Spell

I love a good bath spell, and in this one we will work a bit of glamour magic to boost confidence.

YOU WILL NEED:

3 orange candles

3 pink candles

Cinnamon oil

Biodegradable mica

4 rough chunks rose quartz crystals

2 tablespoons powdered milk

1 teaspoon granulated honey

3 drops neroli oil

3 drops tonka oil

1 coral or orange rose

Tumbled tiger's eye crystal

FURTHER CONSIDERATIONS:

- **Timing:** When the waxing crescent falls on a Tuesday, Friday, or Sunday; in the planetary hour of Mars, Venus, or the sun; or when the moon is in Aries, Leo, or Libra.

- **Attire:** Skyclad.

- **Incense:** Sandalwood.

- **Deity:** Aphrodite/Venus or Artemis/Diana.

- **Affirmation:** "I radiate confidence."

PERFORMING THE SPELL:

1. Anoint each of the candles with cinnamon oil and roll in mica. Arrange the candles in your bathroom in whatever way is appropriate for you.

2. Anchor your bathtub by placing a rose quartz in each of its four corners.

3. Draw your bath, adding the powdered milk, the granulated honey, and 3 drops each of the neroli and tonka oils. Place the rose and the tiger's eye within reach of the tub, then enter the bath.

4. Take hold of the tiger's eye crystal in your palms and cup it to your chest. Say:

> Tiger's eye—stone of confidence and power,
> Lend your magic to me,
> So that my confidence is set free.

5. Drop the crystal into the bath. Now, take hold of the rose and slowly pull off each petal and drop it into the bath as you say:

> By the beauty of this rose,
> I create a more confident me,
> Full of charm and grace.

6. Relax in the bath, focusing on your confidence growing as you luxuriate in the sacred waters you've conjured. When you feel ready, emerge and move forward in confidence.

Enflamed Passion Spell

If you want an abundance of passion in your life, this is the spell for you! It is designed to take action and "make action" by magically influencing the chemistry between you and your partner.

YOU WILL NEED:

Strip of paper

Pen

Dried hibiscus

Patchouli

Dried orchid roots

Small, sharp instrument (like a screw) for carving

Red candle to represent your partner

Cinnamon oil

Second candle (any shape and color) to use for wax

Garnet crystal

Plate

Red roses

Red satin drawstring bag

FURTHER CONSIDERATIONS:

- **Timing:** When the waxing crescent falls on a Tuesday or Friday; in the planetary hour of Mars or Venus; or when the moon is in Scorpio.

- **Attire:** Satin robes, lingerie, red things, or nothing at all.

- **Incense:** Musk and/or patchouli.

- **Deity:** Lilith.

- **Affirmation:** "My partner and I are enflamed in passion."

1. On your strip of paper, write out a petition. Since this is a small strip of paper, you can write "connection" on one side and "passion" on the other. Roll the paper into a tiny scroll. Put aside.

2. Grind your herbs together. Carve out a hole at the bottom of the red candle near the wick, about half an inch deep. Stuff the hole with the scroll and herbs. Add six drops of cinnamon oil to the hole.

3. Light your second candle. Pour its melted wax into the hole in the red candle to seal it. Let the wax harden a bit, but not all the way. Blow out your second candle and set it aside.

4. With the remaining herbs on a flat plate, place the tiny garnet in the center and press the moldable base of the red candle firmly on top of it. Use a slight clockwise motion to ground the candle into the remaining herbal mixture. The result should be an even and flat candle base, with the loaded petition sealed inside the wax with the crystal and herbs.

5. Carve your partner's name along the side of the red candle from base to tip. If you know their birth date or other personal information that helps align the candle to the person, carve that in as well.

6. With the red candle in the center of the plate, dress its stem with the cinnamon oil. Make a ring of red rose petals around the plate, far enough from the candle that they will not catch on fire.

7. Light the candle and chant the following incantation while you visualize the passion that you desire.

> By the power of fire,
> Enflame passion in my desire.

8. Either let the red candle burn all the way down (this will take some time) or blow it out when you feel the time is right and relight it for an hour each day until it is burned out. Once the candle is gone, put any of its remains, the petals, and the herbs into the satin bag and place it under your mattress.

Getting Noticed Spell

This spell is for those individuals who are looking to take action toward gaining attention. Whether for merely superficial reasons, to attract someone you have a crush on, or even to have your hard work recognized in the office, we all need to feel noticed at some point.

YOU WILL NEED:

5 pink candles

Egyptian musk oil

Gold biodegradable mica

Favorite photo of yourself

Silver glitter glue

Pyrite crystal

FURTHER CONSIDERATIONS:

- **Timing:** When the waxing crescent falls on a Friday or Sunday; in the planetary hour of Venus or the sun; or when the moon is in Leo or Libra.

- **Attire:** Pink, gold, or silver.

- **Incense:** Nag champa.

- **Deity:** Aphrodite/Venus or Lilith.

- **Affirmation:** "I am seen and attract the attention I want."

PERFORMING THE SPELL:

1. Anoint the pink candles with Egyptian musk oil and top them off with the gold mica. Anchor them around you in a circle.

2. In a clockwise motion, draw a circle around yourself in the photo with the silver glitter glue. Once done, place the pyrite in the center. Say:

I am bright and glisten with moonlight.

3. Visualize your aura sparkling and glowing at full force. Begin to chant "Notice me" over and over, raising energy in your spell. When finished, blow out the candles.

4. Place your glittered photo in the center of your altar and surround it with the candles. Continue to light them as often as needed or whenever you need a bit of extra attention. For extra oomph, dab a bit of the Egyptian musk oil behind your ears when heading out.

Hurry Up Spell for Impatience

Sometimes it is best to let spells unfold organically and not interfere with timing, since linear time is something that we've created as humans. However, when dealing with matters that have a due date, the following spell can maximize the growing power of the moon for quick, action-packed results.

YOU WILL NEED:

Cinnamon

Black pepper

Chili pepper

Pen

Paper

Charcoal disc

Cauldron or large fireproof bowl

Red candle

FURTHER CONSIDERATIONS:

- **Timing:** When the new moon falls on a Tuesday; in the planetary hour of Mars; or when the moon is in Aries or Scorpio.

- **Attire:** Red.

- **Incense:** Frankincense.

- **Deity:** Khonshu.

- **Affirmation:** "I will get the answer I want soon."

PERFORMING THE SPELL:

1. Grind together all of the spices into a fine powder.

2. Write a petition on the paper identifying the situation for which you need a fast result. Loosely fold the paper.

3. Light the charcoal disc and place it into your cauldron or bowl. Sprinkle the spice mixture on top of it.

4. Pass the folded petition through the smoke and say:

> By the powers of air and fire,
> I ask the moon to speed my desire.

5. Now set the paper aflame and toss it into the cauldron to burn. Meditate on your goals coming to you quickly. Once the charcoal has cooled and you have released your ritual, toss the remains and ashes into the wind, saying:

> May my spell soar through the breeze
> And come to me faster, please.

Making the First Move

An important part of action is being ambitious enough to go after it. This spell involves making a magical oil blend and a diffuser beaded bracelet to wear.

YOU WILL NEED:

Fractionated coconut oil

1 dram bottle

1 dash neroli oil

1 dash rose oil

1 dash ylang-ylang oil

1 drop cinnamon oil

Rhodonite beads

Pyrite beads

3 lava rock beads

Stretchy bead cord

FURTHER CONSIDERATIONS:

- **Timing:** When the waxing crescent falls on a Tuesday or Sunday; in the planetary hour of Mars or Sun; or when the moon is in Aries or Leo.

- **Attire:** Red, orange, yellow, or gold.

- **Incense:** Rose.

- **Deity:** Artemis/Diana.

- **Affirmation:** "I am confident and go after what I want."

1. First, mix your oil blend by pouring the fractionated coconut oil into half of your dram bottle. Next combine it with equal parts of the neroli, rose, and ylang-ylang oils. Add one drop of cinnamon oil. Put the cap on and shake well while you say:

Magic oil, help me find the confidence in me
To make the first move, blessed be!

2. Construct your beaded bracelet by using an even number of beads divided into two sets. Assemble the first set, alternating the rhodonite and pyrite beads. Then add the three lava beads, followed by the second set, alternating as you did the first. Tie off the string. Bless the bracelet, saying:

Crystals of the earth, help instill the confidence in me
To make the first move, blessed be!

3. Anoint the lava beads with your oil blend to conclude the ritual.

Maiden Moon Ritual

This ritual honors the divine lunar goddess, the Maiden, who is associated with action and is often considered the archetypal inquisitive feminine force. She is ambitious and full of life.

Another prominent lunar goddess is Artemis/Diana, the goddess of the hunt and crescent moon, whom you can choose to worship here instead of the Maiden, should she resonate more deeply with your intentions. Even goddesses like Lilith or Hekate would be suitable, as each has a maiden aspect. Please feel free to adapt the ritual as you feel appropriate to fit your personal needs or any existing bonds you have with any deity.

YOU WILL NEED:

Representation of the Maiden (statue, framed photo, art, etc.)

Black candlestick

White or silver candlestick

Vase of fresh white flowers like carnations, roses, gardenias, or lilies

Bowl

Milk

Tumbled moonstone crystal

FURTHER CONSIDERATIONS:

- **Timing:** When the waxing moon is on a Monday; during the planetary hour of the moon; or when the moon is in Cancer.

- **Attire:** White, pink, peach, or pastel colors.

- **Incense:** Amber, rose, or sandalwood.

- **Deity:** Artemis/Diana.

- **Affirmation:** "I honor the Maiden of the moon. I honor her reflection in me."

1. Arrange your moon altar so that your representation of the Maiden is in the center. Place the black candlestick to the left and the white or silver candlestick to the right. The flowers will go behind the Maiden. Place the bowl in front of it.

2. Invite the Maiden into your space. Close your eyes and reach out your arms in a "Y" position up to the moon. Call her down into your space, saying:

> *Virgin goddess glowing bright,*
> *Milky white in the dark of night,*
> *Dance across the sky, Ms. Crescent Moon,*
> *And further come into bloom.*
> *Full of action and ambition,*
> *Join me on this night of witchin'*
> *Reflect your vibrancy in me,*
> *Here and now while I celebrate thee.*

3. Pour the milk into the bowl. Add the moonstone to the milk. Now take one of the white flowers and pull the petals off the flower one by one and drop them into the milk bowl. With each petal, think about the actions you are taking to manifest abundance in your life.

4. Hold the bowl up to the moon as an offering and dedicate it to the Maiden in your own way. Meditate on your inner Maiden charging ahead and going after abundance.

5. Close your ritual and take your bowl outside. Pour it on the earth under the moon as an offering to the Maiden. Collect the moonstone and place it under your pillow for prophetic dreams and visions to help further your abundant actions.

Resolving Conflict

No matter how many crystals and how much sage you have, you are bound to hit an obstacle at one point or another. In this spell, you will work to take charge of the situation and create harmony in the face of adversity.

YOU WILL NEED:

1 black candle with holder

1 white candle with holder

Paper

Pen

Fluorite crystal

Sharp knife

Honey

FURTHER CONSIDERATIONS:

- **Timing:** When the waxing crescent falls on a Friday or Saturday; in the planetary hour of Venus or Saturn; or when the moon is in Taurus, Libra, or Capricorn.

- **Attire:** Black and white.

- **Incense:** Rose.

- **Deity:** Aphrodite/Venus.

- **Affirmation:** "[Name of person or situation] and I are in harmony."

PERFORMING THE SPELL:

1. Set up your space so that your black and white candles are side by side.

2. On the paper, write your name above the situation or person that is creating conflict for you. Place the paper between the candles and place the fluorite crystal on top.

3. Take the black candlestick and turn it upside down. Chip away at the base with the knife so that the wick is exposed. Place it into the holder upside down. Anoint the white candle with a bit of honey. Light both candles and say:

> May *white light and harmony grow in the darkness*
> And *bring amity to me and* [situation or person].

4. Let the candles burn out, collecting any leftover wax and wrapping it in the paper with the crystal. Bury the wax-and-crystal bundle in an area frequented by you and your adversary. When you encounter your adversary, focus on the fact that the conflict is now buried.

Road Opener Spell

This spell is my take on a traditional hoodoo spell called a road opener. It is used to open blockages or obstacles standing in the way of your success.

YOU WILL NEED:

Knife or toothpick

Yellow pillar candle

Road Opener Oil (1 part san-dalwood, 1 part gardenia, 1 part vanilla)

Pyrite crystal dust

Fireproof plate or cauldron

4 bay leaves

4 skeleton keys (easily found at craft stores)

Lemon zest

White or yellow rose

FURTHER CONSIDERATIONS:

- **Timing:** When the waxing crescent falls on a Wednesday, Thursday, or Sunday; in the planetary hour of Mercury, Jupiter, or the sun; or when the moon is in Gemini, Virgo, or Sagittarius.

- **Attire:** Yellow, orange, or gold.

- **Incense:** Sandalwood.

- **Deity:** Hekate.

- **Affirmation:** "The roads are open for new opportunity."

PERFORMING THE SPELL:

1. Carve the shape of a key into the yellow candle and anoint it with the Road Opener oil.

2. Put the pyrite dust in the center of your plate. Using a lighter, gently warm the bottom of the candle so that the wax is malleable. Push the base of the candle into the dust so that the pyrite particles are inserted into the wax. While doing this, say:

> *Pyrite, I ask that you assist in attracting*
> *New opportunities and success my way.*

3. Holding the bay leaves, say:

> *Bay leaves, I ask that you assist in paving the way for*
> *New opportunities and success for me.*

Place a drop of oil on each leaf and place them around the candle so that each point faces a cardinal direction: north, south, east, and west.

4. Hold the skeleton keys and say:

> *Keys, I ask that you assist in unlocking the doors for*
> *New opportunities and success for me.*

Anoint the keys with the oil and visualize success in whichever area of your life you want it coming to you.

5. Now take your lemon zest and sprinkle it in a clockwise motion around the base of the candle, saying:

> *Lemon, I ask that you assist in bringing*
> *New opportunities and success my way.*

6. Take your fresh rose. Remove the head so that a pile of petals remains in your hands. In a clockwise motion, sprinkle them in a circle around the plate, saying:

> *White roses of purity and new beginnings, I ask that you assist in growing*
> *New opportunities and success in my life.*

7. Sit and visualize the roads to success opening around you. When you are ready, extinguish the candle. Reenact step 7 each day until the candle is burned out. Bury any remains.

CHAPTER 5

First Quarter Moon:
Make Decisions

The first quarter moon is a time when the moon's illumination is split directly in half. This half-light, half-dark condition presents a unique time of polarity. Like the crossroads, this is a great time to start making decisions that coincide with the greater good of your intentions. The first quarter is a short phase, occurring for only one day, directly after the seven days of the waxing crescent. Because of this, it is important to do any of your magical work for the first quarter on the exact night of the moon. Review your calendar or the oracle of Google for the exact date and time as it corresponds to your time zone.

POTION

SPELLS/RITUALS/CEREMONIES

Determined Decisions

It is important to make sure that you follow up your magically charged intentions in a practical way. Using the following lines, write down decisions that you have made toward fulfilling your intentions or those you are having trouble making at this time. Some examples may be "I've decided to leave my job" and "I am struggling to make healthier choices." Remember that with every step you take in the mundane world toward your goal, the more momentum your magic has.

_____

_____

_____

_____

_____

Reflect upon the decisions and factors you can continue to contribute toward manifesting abundance in your life. If you feel inclined, utilize this moon phase for spellcasting to help make the right decisions. Following are a moon potion and eight spells designed to assist with just that.

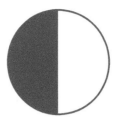

Half-Moon Lavender Latte

For the half-moon, we are mixing coffee and tea to mimic the polarity of light and dark. Coffee and lavender help stimulate the mind and can assist in making mindful decisions. Almond and orange will act as the abundance attractors while promoting alertness.

YOU WILL NEED:

2 to 3 fresh orange peels

Water

1 to 4 shots espresso or strong brewed coffee

2 teaspoons lavender simple syrup

6 ounces almond milk

Pinch culinary rose petals

FURTHER CONSIDERATIONS:

- Instead of using store-bought lavender simple syrup, make your own by combining 1 cup of water, 1 cup of sugar, and 3 tablespoons of culinary lavender in a saucepan. Bring to a boil and then simmer for about 10 minutes until thick. Strain into an airtight container, removing any residual floral bits, and store in the refrigerator to cool and keep fresh.

- Since the moon is still growing to its peak power, drink warm to further stimulate the energies of growth.

1. Add the orange peels into a pot of water and bring to a boil. Turn off the heat and let steep for an hour. Strain the liquid into a separate, sealable container.

2. Pour the coffee into your mug of choice. Add two teaspoons each of the lavender simple syrup and orange peel tea. Stir in a clockwise motion, mimicking the cycle of the moon.

3. Heat the milk and add to the mug. Stir again with intention and garnish with rose petals on top.

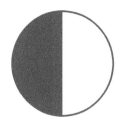

Asking for a Sign

When making decisions, sometimes we come to a crossroads, and here we are going to be making an offering while we call upon the goddess Hekate for assistance. If you are uncomfortable using Hekate, you may remove her name from the invocation and use the moon goddess in general, or another deity with whom you are in league.

YOU WILL NEED:

Sharp cutting knife

1 red apple

2 drops honey

2 bay leaves

2 pins

2 skeleton keys (easily found at craft stores)

4 coins (any denomination)

Red wine in a flask

FURTHER CONSIDERATIONS:

- **Timing:** When the first quarter moon falls on a Wednesday, Thursday, or Saturday; in the planetary hour of Mercury, Jupiter, or Saturn; or when the moon is in Virgo, Sagittarius, or Capricorn.

- **Attire:** Black and white.

- **Incense:** Frankincense.

- **Deity:** Hekate.

- **Affirmation:** "I will know the right way."

PERFORMING THE SPELL:

1. Locate a crossroads. Depending on where you live, you may find a traditional four-way or three-way intersection. If you are accustomed to city life like me, you may find a six-way intersection.

Just make sure you find one that is easily accessible and safe to be alone at during the night, and that you perform your spell away from the flow of traffic (e.g., on a sidewalk).

2. Gather all your supplies and head to the crossroads. When there, perform a pentagram salute. Place your dominant hand at your forehead and trace a line down to your left breast, to your right shoulder, to your left shoulder, to your right breast, and back to your forehead.

3. Take the apple and, with the knife, cut it horizontally so that the apple's "star" is shown. On each half, place a drop of honey in the star, followed by the bay leaf, and then pin it in place. Place the apple pieces on the ground in front of you in a parallel position.

4. Between the apple pieces, place the two keys so that they are in a cross-like shape. Place a coin in each of the open spaces around the keys.

5. Hold the wine to the moon and call upon Hekate, saying:

> *Hekate, moon goddess of the crossroads,*
> *I ask that you lend your powers now,*
> *And help me make a decision regarding*
> [Whatever it is you seek an answer to].
> *May you please accept these sacred things as offerings*
> *In exchange for a sign of which road I should take.*

6. Take a sip of the wine and pour the wine from the flask over the keys in front of you. Pick up the two apple pieces and think hard about the crossroads you are currently at in your life. If you are at a three-way intersection, throw them down the two different roads in front of you. If you are at a four-way intersection or more, throw them down two roads opposite each other.

7. Bow to the moon and offer your thanks. Be on the lookout for a sign that you will know is the answer to your questions. Trust your intuition and move forward in the direction shown.

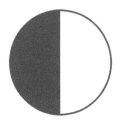

Healthy Habits Spell

This spell can be used to inspire healthier habits.

YOU WILL NEED:

Carving knife

1 potato

Blue candle in jar

Tumbled turquoise stone

1 High John root

Health Oil (1 dash each of neroli and black pepper, with 3 drops of mint)

FURTHER CONSIDERATIONS:

- **Timing:** When the first quarter moon falls on a Thursday, Friday, or Saturday; in the planetary hour of Venus, Jupiter, or Saturn; or when the moon is in Libra, Sagittarius, or Capricorn.

- **Attire:** Blue or red.

- **Incense:** Dragon's blood.

- **Deity:** Aphrodite/Venus.

- **Affirmation:** "I am happy, healthy, and free."

PERFORMING THE SPELL:

1. Carve a hole in the potato large enough to fit the turquoise and root. As you do this, focus on the time and efforts you will be putting into being healthy.

2. Light the blue candle and meditate on the healthier you and the decisions you can make to help that vision become a reality. Let the candle burn so that you have a fair amount of liquid wax buildup.

3. Push the crystal and root into the hole in the potato and remain focused on your idea of the healthiest you possible. Now, place five drops of the Health Oil into the hole, and top it off by pouring the liquid wax into the hole to seal it shut. Wait for the wax to cool.

4. Go outside in an undisturbed, safe location. Dig a hole large enough to cover the potato completely. Place the potato inside and, while burying it, say:

Half-moon in the sky,
Help me in my decision to be healthy and free.
I welcome my healthiness and bury the heaviness of bad choices.

Mental Clarity Spell

This is a very simple spell that you can perform when you are looking for a bit of a mental tune-up.

YOU WILL NEED:

Pillow

Yoga mat (optional)

Large white candle

3 drops lemon oil

3 drops lavender oil

Amethyst crystal

FURTHER CONSIDERATIONS:

- **Timing:** When the first quarter moon falls on a Wednesday; in the planetary hour of Mercury; or when the moon is in Gemini or Virgo.

- **Attire:** Purple or white.

- **Incense:** Lavender.

- **Music:** Play soft, meditative music or binary beats that stimulate mental clarity.

- **Affirmation:** "My mind is clear and focused."

PERFORMING THE SPELL:

1. Arrange your space so that you can easily lie down in front of your moon altar. Bring a pillow, a yoga mat, and anything else that helps you lie down in ease. Set a timer for 30 minutes.

2. Place the candle in the center of your altar. Anoint it with three drops of each oil.

3. Light the candle and say:

> *Lemon and lavender, powerful flame,*
> *Grant me peace of mind and free me from disdain.*

4. Hold the amethyst between your palms and say:

> *Purple crystal from the earth,*
> *Help bring clarity to me at this time.*

5. Lie back and allow your head to rest on the pillow. Place the amethyst crystal on your forehead between your eyes—your third eye. Close your eyes and allow yourself to drift out of the space you are currently in and into total relaxation.

6. Once done, blow out the candle and let the smoke ascend into the atmosphere of your space. Relight it whenever you need a little recharge.

Pivot Spell

Not everything goes the way you think it will. Sometimes life takes a sharp turn off course, and you either back up and get back on the road or change course completely. Regardless of which way you go, I've learned it's best to just enjoy the scenery of whatever detour you take. This spell is designed to help you pivot and do just that.

YOU WILL NEED:

Small piece of blue paper

Blue pen

Black paper

White paper

Cauldron or fireproof bowl

FURTHER CONSIDERATIONS:

- **Timing:** When the first quarter moon falls on a Thursday; in the planetary hour of Jupiter; or when the moon is in Sagittarius.

- **Attire:** Blue or red.

- **Incense:** Frankincense.

- **Deity:** Lilith.

- **Affirmation:** "I am unrooted and move in the way that is meant for me."

PERFORMING THE SPELL:

1. On one side of the blue paper, write down the course you have been on. On the other side, write the new challenge or obstacle that has come up that requires you to make a decision.

2. Place the blue paper between the black and white papers. Fold the edges of the black and white papers lightly so that the blue one remains inside. Light the papers on fire and toss them into your cauldron or fireproof bowl, saying:

> *First quarter moon, help me see which way is meant to be*
> *So that I may pivot accordingly.*

3. Let the ashes cool, then take them outside. Toss them to the wind and have faith that you are on the right path.

Seven of Cups Tarot Spell

The seven of cups is a tarot card that symbolizes an abundance of choices. This spell will use the card to address where you should focus right now. There are many different illustrations on the seven of cups card; for this spell it is important to use the Rider-Waite deck.

YOU WILL NEED:

Seven of cups Rider-Waite tarot card

Blue candle

Labradorite crystal

FURTHER CONSIDERATIONS:

- **Timing:** When the first quarter moon falls on a Monday; in the planetary hour of the moon; or when the moon is in Cancer.

- **Attire:** Blue or black.

- **Incense:** Jasmine or lavender.

- **Deity:** Hekate or Lilith.

- **Affirmation:** "Among many choices, I choose with my intuition."

PERFORMING THE SPELL:

1. Place your seven of cups upside down in front of the lit blue candle. Holding the labradorite, say:

By power of moon and stone,
I ask for the best choice to be shown.

2. Place the crystal on top of the card. Close your eyes, and focus on your intuitive powers.

3. Remove the crystal from the card and flip the card over. Shift your sight in and out of focus on the card in front of you. Which of the cups are you most drawn to?

- **Castle:** Shows adventure. It can suggest that right now you need to focus on maximizing your abundance by saying yes to everything. Carpe diem—seize the day—and seize the abundance in your life.
- **Cloaked figure:** Signifies spirituality. Now is the time to work with your spirit guides and higher self to become attuned with the magic of the world around you.
- **Dragon:** A symbol of fear. This is a time for you to focus on your mental well-being and what might be holding you back from achieving abundance in your life.
- **Head:** Represents love. Now is a time for you to be full of love. Think about how you show love to others and yourself and how you can become a magnet for more abundance by opening your heart to the universe.
- **Snake:** Occult wisdom. Now is the time to focus on your magical studies and the esoteric arts. It may also indicate that you need to pay attention to your sexuality and expressing it rather than suppressing it.
- **Jewels:** Showcases prosperity. Right now is a time to focus on getting your finances in order and establish a better relationship with materialistic abundance.
- **Wreath:** A symbol of victory and validation. This cup beckons you to keep up the hustle and continue to chase the success you are after. However, unlike the other cups, there is a skull reflected in the cup, denoting egotistical success that may hurt your reputation and friendships. Remember to focus on success through being of service rather than personal gain.

4. Focus on the cup that you are drawn to and how its representation mirrors the situations in your life. If possible, meditate or reflect on this daily until you have achieved the intentions indicated by the card.

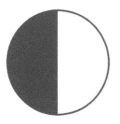

Spell to Influence the Decision of Another

Every now and then you will find yourself at the mercy of another person's decision. The following spell helps set a fire under the individual you need an answer from. This spell is fueled by the intent that the decision will ultimately be for the highest good of all involved. Here we will be creating a poppet, or magical doll, which is usually made from a variety of ingredients, such as corn, fabric, and other materials. Poppets are routinely used in folk magic to represent a specific person associated with a spell.

YOU WILL NEED:

Gingerbread man cookie cutter

White fabric

Fabric scissors

3 sewing needles

Thread

Photo of individual

Cinnamon

Black pepper

Stuffing

4 blue candles

4 quartz crystals

Honey

Photo of you

FURTHER CONSIDERATIONS:

- **Timing:** When the first quarter moon falls on a Tuesday or Wednesday; in the planetary hour of Mars or Mercury; or when the moon is in Aries, Gemini, or Aquarius.

- **Attire:** Red, black, or pink.

- **Incense:** Frankincense.

- **Deity:** Hekate or Lilith.

- **Affirmation:** "I influence the decisions of [name of person]."

1. Trace a gingerbread man cookie cutter on the fabric in two locations. Cut out the figures with fabric scissors.

2. Using a needle and thread, begin to stitch the outer borders of the cutouts together, leaving an opening on one of the sides to stuff with some of the other ingredients.

3. Scrunch up the photo of the person and stuff it into the doll with the spices and stuffing. Sew it shut and place the doll in the center of your altar.

4. Around the doll, make a circle with the four candles and quartz pieces, alternating candle and crystal. Light the candles and visualize the person represented by the doll.

5. Dip all three needles into the honey. Then push them one by one into the head of the doll, saying:

Like the sweetness of honey,
I will be on [full name of person]*'s mind.*
By one, this spell has begun.
By two, this doll is you.
By three, the decision will best affect me.

6. Place the cut-out photo of yourself on the needles, which will act as the legs holding it up. Say:

While I'm on your mind, [full name of person],
the decision of [what you are after] *is what you'll see.*
For the good of all, but most for me,
It is with my will that a favorable verdict will be.

7. Leave the doll on your altar. Each week, return and repeat steps 5 and 6, using fresh honey, until a decision has been made. Bury the doll once the spell has been completed.

To Stay or Go Pendulum Spell

Do you stay in the relationship, or do you humbly bow out? Do you continue in the dead-end job or break free and find something more suited to your needs? This spell will assist in helping the universe pull you in the direction that is most suitable for you right now. Sometimes, as bad as things are, we haven't learned the lesson we need yet. To help determine the answer, you will witch-*craft* your own pendulum.

YOU WILL NEED:

A crystal point

Jeweler's wire or string

A lightweight chain or cord

Image of your dilemma (e.g., a photo of you and your significant other; your company's logo or stationery with its letterhead; etc.)

Bowl of cold spring water

3 pinches rock salt

FURTHER CONSIDERATIONS:

- **Timing:** When the first quarter moon falls on a Wednesday; in the planetary hour of Mercury; or when the moon is in Gemini or Virgo.

- **Attire:** Purple or white.

- **Incense:** Amber.

- **Deity:** Hekate.

- **Affirmation:** "I will choose the right way."

1. It is best to begin the preparations for this ritual a few days to a week before the night you plan to work it. First, select a crystal point that you are most drawn to. One of the best ways to do this is to visit a store that sells crystals. You may eyeball a few that interest you. Hold your dominant hand a few inches away from the selected crystals and gently wave your hand over the area until you feel pulled by one of them. Whichever crystal you are pulled to is the point that you should use for the pendulum.

2. Wrap the jeweler's wire or string around the crystal and your chain or cord so that when you hold it, the point of the crystal will go downward.

3. Cleanse your newly created pendulum by dipping it in cold spring water that has been mixed with three pinches of rock salt. Stir the pendulum in the mixture and ask that it be cleansed and purified in preparation for your work.

4. Once your pendulum has been created, begin to ask questions that you know the answers to. For instance, I might say, "Is my name Michael?" or something of the like. When asking, hold the point steady and let go without forcibly moving the tool. As you ask the question and focus on it, pay attention to the movements of the point. A horizontal swing will signify yes, vertical no, and circular neutral.

5. Once the pendulum is calibrated to your energy, place a photo that represents the theme of your question on your altar. Ground and center yourself, focusing on the circumstances surrounding your questions. Hold and steady the pendulum over the photo and ask it to reveal an answer to you. If you are getting only neutral responses, this will signify that now is not the time for action; instead, wait and try again later.

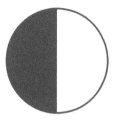

Truth Spell

Sometimes you just need to get to the bottom of a situation to better understand how to move forward. The following spell is used to get to the bottom of a situation and expose an abundance of truth.

YOU WILL NEED:

Photo of person whom you suspect of committing fraud

Glass plate

Sea salt

3 nails

Patchouli oil

Sage oil

Blue or white candle with holder

FURTHER CONSIDERATIONS:

- **Timing:** When the waxing crescent moon falls on a Wednesday; in the planetary hour of Mercury; or when the moon is in Gemini or Sagittarius.

- **Attire:** Blue or white.

- **Incense:** Frankincense or sandalwood.

- **Deity:** Lilith.

- **Affirmation:** "I hear only the truth."

1. Place the photo in the center of the plate. Over the photo, draw an infinity symbol (which looks like a horizontal 8) with the salt. Salt is used for cleansing, and the infinity symbol can be used to represent equality in truth and justice.

2. Anoint each nail with the oils. As you push the nails into the candle, one-by-one, say:

> By one, you will speak to me.
> By two, truth will come from you.
> By three, deceptions I shall hear and see.

3. Place the candle in the candleholder on top of the photo and salt. Light the candle and say:

> I seek to know the truth from your lips.
> As this candle burns it will bubble up to your tongue's tip.

4. Let the candle burn completely out. Discard the remains and start asking the questions you seek answers to.

CHAPTER 6

Waxing Gibbous Moon: *Get Specific*

As the moon becomes fuller, we transition from the first quarter and into the waxing gibbous phase. During this time, the moon starts to appear brighter and fuller in the sky. Like the waxing crescent, this phase lasts for seven days and provides a unique time for homing in on your intentions, dreams, and goals. The closer the moon gets to reaching full power, the better the time is to do everything, both magically and practically, to go after your goals and manifest your targeted desires into reality.

POTION

SPELLS/RITUALS/CEREMONIES

Refining Your Intentions

The waxing gibbous phase is the final state of the moon cycle before its full potency is reached. Because of this, you should work on strengthening and refining your intentions. It is time to get really specific about the abundance you are seeking. Using the following lines, write out your targeted and achievable specifications and reflect upon them. Examples could be something along the lines of "I want $5,000" instead of "I want more money." Or "I want to be in an exclusive, monogamous relationship with [XYZ]" rather than "I want a relationship."

_____

_____

_____

_____

_____

    The potion and eight spells that make up the remainder of this chapter span a variety of topics focused on strengthening your intentions. As you reflect on the seeds you have planted, feel free to work any of these spells or adapt as you see fit.

Hot Moony Potion

A Hot Moony is my witchy take on a Hot Toddy. It combines the sweetness needed for attracting abundance and the spicy heat that reflects the growing moon.

YOU WILL NEED:

1 piece fresh ginger (4 cm long)

2 cinnamon sticks

4 cups water

1 ounce whiskey or bourbon

1 tablespoon honey

2 teaspoons lemon juice

1 vanilla bean

FURTHER CONSIDERATIONS:

- For a nonalcoholic version, substitute black tea for the whiskey.

- Refrigerate the ginger cinnamon tea and reheat on the stove or in the microwave for an additional serving.

- Enjoy hot, remembering that heat stimulates growth as we accelerate further toward the full moon.

PREPARING THE POTION:

1. Peel and slice the ginger root. Place it in a saucepan with the cinnamon sticks and water. Bring to a boil and reduce the heat to low, simmering for 5 to 10 minutes. Remove from the heat and set aside to cool; steep for 5 to 10 minutes depending on how strong a taste you'd like.

2. Strain the potion into a mug or desired cup. Add the alcohol, honey, and lemon juice. Stir in a clockwise motion.

3. Slice the side of the vanilla bean and scrape the inner powder into the potion. Stir again and enjoy.

Archetype Personification Spell

Another form of moon magic is slipping into the personification of an archetype with whom you want to align. This is a super fun spell and requires a lot of visualization to manifest accurately. Before you begin, think about some archetypes that you are drawn to.

YOU WILL NEED:

Photo of yourself

Photo of your desired persona

An outfit or multiple outfits that highlights your chosen

archetype (you will not be wearing this to perform the spell; rather, you will use this *as part of* the spell)

Labradorite crystal

FURTHER CONSIDERATIONS:

- **Timing:** When the waxing gibbous moon is on a Friday; in the planetary hour of Venus; or when the moon is in Libra.

- **Attire:** Skyclad.

- **Incense:** Rose.

- **Deity:** Aphrodite/Venus or Lilith.

- **Affirmation:** "I am [name of persona]."

PERFORMING THE SPELL:

1. Think about who you are attracted to. This can be a celebrity, character, or overall archetype, like the seductress, warrior, hero, bombshell, etc. Once you have determined this, print a photo of the character.

2. Glue the photo of yourself directly on top of the photo of your archetype. Once dried, place this on top of your chosen clothing, saying:

Merged together you and me,
May others see who I want to be.

3. Now take the labradorite in your palms. Cup it to the moon and say:

Growing moon, bless this crystal of transformation.
May it assist me in personifying _____.

4. Place the stone on top of the photos and leave it to charge all night. In the morning, dress in your chosen clothing and carry the crystal on you while you visualize yourself as the character you have selected.

Better Communication Spell

Sometimes it can be hard to find your voice in a world that would often rather you remain silent. This next spell involves you making a communication talisman. Wear the finished piece as close to your throat as possible to stimulate your chakra of communication.

YOU WILL NEED:

Turquoise crystal   Cord or chain

Crystal cage

FURTHER CONSIDERATIONS:

- **Timing: When the waxing gibbous moon is on a Wednesday; in the planetary hour of Mercury; or when the moon is in Gemini or Virgo.**

- **Attire: Blue.**

- **Incense: Frankincense.**

- **Deity: Artemis/Diana or Yemaya.**

- **Affirmation: "I communicate effortlessly."**

PERFORMING THE SPELL:

1. Hold the stone to the moon. Call forth the lunar energy, asking:

    Glowing sphere in the sky, I ask that you bless my voice with perfect speech so that I may communicate effectively and efficiently.

2. Now push the crystal into the cage wiring. Add the cord or chain and hold it so that it dangles in front of your mouth. Purse your lips and blow a long, deep, and focused breath onto the crystal. Say:

> *With my breath you link to me,*
> *Unlock my voice and set it free*
> *So that I can communicate more easily.*

3. Place the necklace around your neck. Hold it with your dominant hand against your throat and create a purring sound to help harmonize the crystal to your throat. Thank the moon and move forward in perfect trust that your communication will blossom into perfection.

Body Positivity Mirror Spell

Here is a self-love spell to help create healing thoughts for those struggling with body acceptance or body dysmorphia.

YOU WILL NEED:

6 pink or orange candles

Pink rose

Unscented lotion

Oil blend (equal parts rose, musk, and sandalwood)

Hand mirror

FURTHER CONSIDERATIONS:

- **Timing:** When the waxing gibbous moon falls on Friday; in the planetary hour of Venus; or when the moon is in Taurus.

- **Attire:** Skyclad.

- **Incense:** Rose and sandalwood.

- **Deity:** Aphrodite/Venus.

- **Affirmation:** "I am beauty incarnate, inside and out."

PERFORMING THE SPELL:

1. Stand in the center of the six lit candles. One by one, pick off a petal from the rose as you walk the perimeter of the circle in a clockwise motion, chanting the affirmation.

2. Place a dollop of lotion in your hands with three drops of the oil. Mix with your hands and begin to slowly massage the lotion into your body as you say, "I love you."

3. Hold the mirror and say:

> *Standing here in this circle, painted in self-love,*
> *I am pure, perfect, and beautiful in my natural state.*
> *I love myself. I love myself. I love myself.*

Feel the love around you and celebrate yourself in this moment.

4. After the ritual, collect the petals, dress in a coat or robe, and head outside. Throw the petals into the sky so that they rain down upon you in the moonlight. Feel at peace with yourself and know that you are a divine expression of beauty.

Moon Muse Painting Spell for Inspiration

The following spell is a dose of practical magic to help ignite inspiration.

YOU WILL NEED:

4 fluorite crystals

Yellow candle

Lemon oil

Dried lavender

Paintbrushes

Set of paints (acrylic or watercolor)

Canvas or appropriate paper for the paints you are using

FURTHER CONSIDERATIONS:

- **Timing:** When the waxing gibbous moon falls on a Monday or Friday; in the planetary hour of the moon or Venus; or when the moon is in Libra or Pisces.

- **Attire:** Wear anything that makes you feel creative and free.

- **Incense:** Frankincense.

- **Affirmation:** "I conjure creativity and unleash it from me."

PERFORMING THE SPELL:

1. Anchor your space's boundary with a crystal in each of the four cardinal directions.

2. Anoint the yellow candle with lemon oil to help remove blockages to your creativity. Roll it in the dried lavender, light it, and say:

Here and now, I conjure the creativity in me.
In this sacred space, may inspiration be set free.

3. Close your eyes and focus on the area where you are looking for inspiration.

4. With your eyes still closed, dip your brush into the color that calls most to you. Put it to the canvas or paper and let your creativity flow instinctively. If you see something in your mind, paint it. If you just want to doodle and make lines, do it, picking up different colors as you are called to. While you paint, chant, "I conjure creativity and unleash it from me."

5. Place the finished piece on your altar to further accumulate magic and meaning.

Reclaim Personal Power

Life's obstacles can sometimes drag us down and make us feel less than empowered. So let's smash those feelings and reclaim personal power with this simple spell.

YOU WILL NEED:

Knife or toothpick

5 candles (green, yellow, red, blue, and white)

4 bay leaves

Cinnamon oil

1 High John root

FURTHER CONSIDERATIONS:

- **Timing:** When the waxing gibbous moon falls on a Tuesday; in the planetary hour of Mars; or when the moon is in Aries.

- **Attire:** White or skyclad.

- **Incense:** Dragon's blood.

- **Deity:** Lilith.

- **Affirmation:** "I am strong and powerful."

1. Using the chart, carve the elemental symbol into each corresponding candle:

COLOR	ELEMENT	DIRECTION	SYMBOL
Green	Earth	North	Upside-down triangle with horizontal line through it
Yellow	Air	East	Triangle with horizontal line through it
Red	Fire	South	Triangle
Blue	Water	West	Upside-down triangle
White	Spirit	Center	Circle

2. Place one bay leaf at each of the cardinal direction points of the circle. Anchor these with the corresponding candles. Dress the candles with cinnamon oil and light them, moving in a clockwise direction. Sit in the center of the circle with the white candle in front of you. Add a drop of oil to the High John root and hold it to your heart, repeating these words:

> By earth, air, water, and fire,
> I call forth my personal power to transpire.
> Elements of the world combine.
> I reclaim my power and let it shine.

3. Visualize yourself being encircled by white light. Meditate on your successes and feel empowered by your accomplishments. Carry the High John root with you when you need a reminder that you are the baddest witch in town.

Richcraft Prosperity Spell

This potent spell is good for manifesting richcraft realness! To manifest your monetary magic, we will be making a mojo bag—a hoodoo-style charm that involves using an assortment of herbs, minerals, and animal biology to achieve a desire.

YOU WILL NEED:

Deposit slip from your bank

Gold ink pen

Metallic gold or yellow drawstring pouch

Faux money

Dried mint

Dried basil

1 bay leaf

1 vanilla bean

1 tonka bean

Pyrite crystal

Lock of your hair

Cinnamon oil

FURTHER CONSIDERATIONS:

- **Timing:** When the waxing gibbous moon falls on a Thursday, Saturday, or Sunday; in the planetary hour of Jupiter, Saturn, or Sun; or when the moon is in Taurus, Leo, or Capricorn.

- **Attire:** Green, gold, or silver.

- **Incense:** Amber or musk.

- **Deity:** Nanna/Sin.

- **Affirmation:** "I am recharged and potent."

PERFORMING THE SPELL:

1. With a gold pen, fill out your bank's deposit slip with various amounts of money that you would like to see being deposited into your account.

2. Fold the deposit slip four times, since four represents structure and foundation. You want to create a more financially stable situation for yourself. Focus on this. Place the deposit slip into the bag while you say:

> *I am prosperous, I am rich,*
> *I call more money to this witch.*

3. Cut the faux money into little bits, creating more and more of it. While you do this, say:

> *Double, double, more money for me.*
> *Prosperity grows toward me.*

4. Now add the dried mint and basil, bay leaf, and vanilla and tonka beans to the bag, saying:

> *Plants of attraction, abundance, and prosperity,*
> *Bring more money to me!*

5. Add the pyrite, saying:

> *Crystal of attraction, abundance, and prosperity,*
> *Bring more money to me!*

6. Lastly, add a lock of your hair, saying:

> *This spell is linked directly to me.*
> *May the money growth be what I see.*

7. Hold the opening of the bag to your mouth and push a long, soft breath of air into the bag, bringing it to life. Tie the bag shut and anoint it with the cinnamon oil.

8. Carry the bag on your person. Anoint it with the cinnamon oil once a week while you visualize more money filling your account. Once you feel you have achieved the prosperity you've desired, bury the bag and give thanks to the universe for your material abundance.

Strengthen Love Spell

The following spell should be used when you are in a trusting, loving relationship with a consenting partner. It should not be used after a fight or as a means to cover up or fix what isn't working. It should be used when you are both 100 percent madly in love with each other and looking to elevate your relationship to the next level.

YOU WILL NEED:

2 dolls that represent both of you (Barbie or Ken dolls work just fine)

Hair from both you and your partner

Shoebox or decorative wooden box that will fit both dolls

Glue

Mirrored tiles

Rose oil

Rose quartz crystal

2 dried roses (even better if they were given to you by your beloved)

Red yarn or thick ribbon

Tokens or other mementos collected throughout your relationship

Dried hibiscus

2 tonka beans

FURTHER CONSIDERATIONS:

- **Timing:** When the waxing gibbous moon is on a Friday; in the planetary hour of Venus; or when the moon is in Taurus or Libra.

- **Attire:** Pink and red.

- **Incense:** Rose.

- **Deity:** Aphrodite/Venus or Yemaya.

- **Affirmation:** "My partner and I are bound and strong in our love."

1. First and foremost, find two dolls that are similar in appearance to you and your partner. These can be Barbies, G. I. Joes—whatever you are drawn to. Have fun with the selection.

2. You need to gather biology from your partner. The easiest to obtain without knowledge is hair from your lover's brush or razor.

3. Decorate the dolls accordingly—add any distinguishing marks or tattoos to them, and stuff any of the biology in the cracks and crevices of their heads, arms, etc.

4. Line your box by gluing the mirrored tiles inside of it to reflect and magnify the love you and your partner share.

5. Drop the oil on the forehead and chest of each doll. Position them together in the box facing each other, with the rose quartz and two roses between them. Begin to wrap the red yarn or ribbon around the dolls, binding them together. As you do this, say:

> I *bind the love shared between* [name of partner] *and me*
> *So that we continue to grow stronger in our love and remain happy.*

6. Tie a tight knot and begin to bind the love of you and your partner:

> *With this knot and the power of our love,*
> *We are blessed and bound by the growing moon above.*

7. Add the remaining mementos, hibiscus, and tonka beans to the box. Store it in a safe place where it will not be disturbed. Continue to add to it as often as you see fit. Each time you add another keepsake, reflect upon the love you share and the happiness you and your partner feel. The more you add, the more and more your love will grow. In the event that you and your lover part ways, remove the dolls and burn the box (in a safe, wide-open space) to release the love binding.

Vision Board Reality Spell

A vision board is a popular tool used to conjure inspiration to help support your goals. These collaged art pieces are seen as useful artifacts for motivating and manifesting your desired future and ultimately obtaining your goals. So let's get specific about how you want the future to unfold and create a vision board to match the goals you are working toward.

YOU WILL NEED:

4 silver candles

4 gold candles

Vanilla oil

Magazines

Scissors

Mortar and pestle

Cinnamon powder

Dried rose petals

Dried mint

Dried lavender

1 vanilla bean

Liquid glue

Paintbrush

Whiteboard

FURTHER CONSIDERATIONS:

- **Timing:** When the waxing gibbous moon falls on a Saturday or Sunday; in the planetary hour of Saturn; or when the moon is in Capricorn or Pisces.

- **Attire:** Silver, gold, or blue.

- **Incense:** Lavender or amber.

- **Deity:** Any.

- **Affirmation:** "My future is constructed through perfect vision."

1. Begin by setting up your ritual space with all the materials needed for your witch-crafting. Place the four silver candles in each of the cardinal directions and the gold ones between each of them. Anoint each candle with the vanilla oil to stimulate attraction and bliss. Light the candles, moving clockwise, and think about your future goals and the visuals that represent them.

2. Holding the magazines, specify your intentions into the world by repeating:

From these pages, I construct my reality.

3. Intuitively flip through the magazines. Pay attention to not only the illustrations but the fonts, texts, and advertisements. Cut out everything that is appealing and aesthetically matches the future you wish to construct. Too much is never enough.

4. Once you have a pile of clippings, sort through them and begin to lay them out in a variety of positions. As you do this, chant the affirmation until you have a collage structure that you feel best represents the vision you have. Any leftover clippings can be discarded.

5. In a mortar and pestle or other grinder, place the cinnamon, rose petals, mint, and lavender. Using a knife, slit the vanilla bean down its side and scoop out the powder. Add it to the other dried herbs and grind them into a fine dust while you focus on attracting the future you want.

6. Add the liquid glue to a bowl, slowly mix in the herbal powder, and stir clockwise. Using a brush, add the glue to the board and layer with your clippings.

7. Once complete, reflect upon the imagery and the steps you plan to take in the real world to achieve your goals. Place the finished board in the window to capture the reflection of the moon's glow overnight. Once charged, hang in a spot that you will see every day and reflect on making your vision a reality.

CHAPTER 7

Full Moon:
Celebrate, Glow, and Reflect

Up to this point we have focused on planting the seeds of our intentions and letting them grow. Now we have reached full bloom with the full moon! Here is where we bask in the luminescence of the moon's peak power. This phase is the perfect time for celebration and reflecting the beauty of the moon in your own magnetic aura. Remember that abundance comes in many forms, and celebrating the moon's glory will only help in attracting and pulling more abundance to you. So, get ready to turn it up . . . because we are about to get lit with lunar energy.

POTION

SPELLS/RITUALS/CEREMONIES

Moon Merrymaking

The power of the full moon is incredible. It is a free-for-all of abundance and energy. On the following lines, write down the success you've achieved from your moon magic so far and what parts of your life you wish to celebrate now. If you feel as though any of your intentions have not manifested, write out those you wish to revisit and refine.

_____

_____

_____

_____

_____

Like the other chapters, the pages that follow include a variety of spells specific to the celebratory energies of the full moon. However, due to the pure potency of this lunar phase, feel free to rework any spells that are not working in your favor now. While it is usually best to cast only one spell at a time, if you are up for some BWE (big witch energy), these spells can be integrated together for a full night of full moon magic.

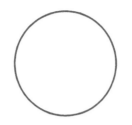

Lunar Drop Martini

This is my twist on a classic lemon drop, adding rosewater or rose simple syrup, a bubbly champagne topper, and a ball of ice to give off that full moon aesthetic. Both lemons and roses are sacred to moon magic, and a bit of bubbly is the perfect addition to your full moon celebrations.

YOU WILL NEED:

Ice ball or cubes

1½ ounces limoncello

1½ ounces gin or vodka

2 teaspoons rosewater or rose simple syrup

Splash of champagne

Lemon twist and/or rose petals to garnish

OPTIONAL:

Sugar for rimming

1 cup water

1 cup sugar

½ cup culinary rose petals

Strainer

Airtight container

FURTHER CONSIDERATIONS:

- For a mocktail version, substitute lemonade for alcoholic ingredients.

- Rim the martini glass with sugar for extra sweetness.

- Instead of using store-bought rosewater or simple syrup, make your own by combining 1 cup of water, 1 cup of sugar, and ½ cup of culinary rose petals in a saucepan. Bring to a boil and then simmer for about 10 minutes until thick. Strain into an airtight container, removing any residual floral bits, and store in the refrigerator to cool and keep fresh.

PREPARING THE POTION:

1. Add the ice ball or cubes to a frosted martini glass.

2. Fill a cocktail shaker with ice and add the limoncello, gin or vodka, and simple syrup. Shake vigorously and strain into the martini glass.

3. Top with the champagne and garnish with a lemon twist or rose petals. Raise a toast to the full moon and enjoy.

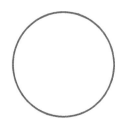

Drawing Down the Moon

Drawing Down the Moon is a ceremonial practice that is performed in a number of Wiccan and neo-pagan traditions. This ritual is designed to honor and worship the mother aspect of the triple goddess. It is a form of hypnosis to surrender yourself to the magic of the moon, celebrating the goddess in her peak phase and reflecting upon her enchanting beauty.

YOU WILL NEED:

2 white or silver candlesticks

A moonstone or selenite crystal

Pink and white floral offerings like roses, gardenias, or stargazer lilies

Fresh fruit offerings like lemons, oranges, strawberries, apples, pears, or figs

White pillar candle

Full Moon Oil (equal parts sandalwood, jasmine, vanilla, and rose)

Silver mica

Lunar Drop Martini (see page 120)

FURTHER CONSIDERATIONS:

- **Timing:** When the full moon falls on a Monday; in the planetary hour of the moon; or when the moon is in Cancer.

- **Attire:** Silver, white, deep pinks, or skyclad.

- **Incense:** Jasmine, rose, or gardenia.

- **Deity:** Selene/Luna, Hekate, or Lilith.

- **Affirmation:** "I am the power of the moon."

1. Decorate your altar space with all of the ingredients.

2. Anoint your white pillar candle with the Full Moon Oil blend and roll it in the silver mica. Light the candle and stand with your arms outstretched above you in the shape of a "Y." Recite the following incantation:

> *Upon this night, when the moon is full,*
> *I honor your greatness, and feel your pull.*
> *Oh silver orb in the sky above, I draw you down with all my love.*
> *May your silver rays of abundance and power,*
> *Pour into me on this very hour.*
> *Celestial mother, great goddess of the moon,*
> *I honor you in your full bloom!*
> *May you fill me with your beauty and grace,*
> *As I surrender before your glowing face.*
> *Through my worship, I connect to thee*
> *And am charged with your cosmic energy.*
> *I acknowledge your luminescence within and around me.*
> *Standing in your sight, engulfed in your bright light,*
> *Ebbing and flowing with the universal forces of magic as your moonchild.*
> *Blessed be!*

3. Holding your crystal in your hands, sit and meditate on the moon and the mother goddess. Write down any revelations or visions you have in your journal to reflect on later. You may feel a spark of energy to dance, chant, or sing out in celebration. Move with this and surrender to the call of the moon.

4. Raise your Lunar Drop Martini or other libation to the moon and drink in honor of the moon. Once the ritual has concluded, take the fruit offerings outside and place them in the full moon light as an offering to the goddess.

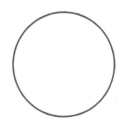

Dream Visions Spell

The full moon is known for being a time when our natural psychic abilities heighten and we have a better chance to connect with our intuition. With this spell, we are going to work on harnessing the intuitive magic of the moon to create vibrant psychic dreams.

YOU WILL NEED:

Labradorite crystal

1 tablespoon dried lavender

1 tablespoon dried mugwort

A drawstring purple or silver bag

3 drops lavender oil

Journal

FURTHER CONSIDERATIONS:

- **Timing:** When the full moon falls on a Monday; in the planetary hour of the moon; or when the moon is in Cancer or Pisces.

- **Attire:** Purple, silver, white, or skyclad.

- **Incense:** Jasmine or gardenia.

- **Deity:** Selene/Luna, Hekate, or Lilith.

- **Music:** Play ambient songs or binary beats to help stimulate your dreams.

- **Affirmation:** "Psychic dreams come to me."

1. At your altar, construct your psychic dream sachet by adding the labradorite, lavender, and mugwort to the drawstring pouch. Tie the bag shut and hold it in your left palm.

2. With your right hand, place three drops of lavender oil onto the bag. Shake it up a bit and take it to your bed with a journal or your Book of Shadows.

3. Get comfortable in bed and shake up the bag a bit more. Give it a big, deep inhalation and smell the enchanting lavender fragrance. Place it under your pillow and drift off to sleep. Upon waking, jot down any memories of dreams you have and try to discern what the symbols, places, or situations mean to you.

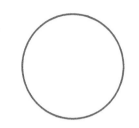

Full Moon Crystal Grid

Crystal grids are as magical as they are beautiful. If you are new to crystal grids, they are essentially a grouping of crystals that have been positioned into a sacred geometric pattern. Once erected, the grid is activated by your intention and fills the space with the combined energies of the crystals. Here we will use the magic of mineralogy to amplify an abundance of lunar energy.

YOU WILL NEED:

White candles

Rose oil

1 moonstone crystal (best if in a sphere shape)

5 chunks selenite

5 quartz points

White rose petals

FURTHER CONSIDERATIONS:

- **Timing:** When the full moon falls on a Monday; in the planetary hour of the moon; or when the moon is in Cancer.

- **Attire:** White, silver, or skyclad.

- **Incense:** Gardenia or jasmine.

- **Deity:** Selene/Luna, Hekate, or Lilith.

- **Affirmation:** "I energize my space with lunar essence."

PERFORMING THE RITUAL:

1. Decorate your space with white candles anointed in rose oil to set the moon magic mood.

2. To construct the grid, place the moonstone in the center of your altar. Place the pieces of selenite in a ring around the moonstone. Now place the quartz points in between each selenite piece and

the moonstone. Have the points face inward toward the moonstone. Lastly, place the rose petals around the entire formation you have made.

3. Now the grid needs to be activated. To do so you will channel your intent by tracing a pattern over the crystals. Essentially, the pattern is weaving in and out so that each crystal is connected by the intent you are fueling it with. Your activator can be anything you prefer to direct energy with. This can be an athame, a lit candle, an incense stick, a talisman or pendant, a pendulum, or even just your index finger.

4. Holding your activator over the moonstone, close your eyes and focus on the beauty of the full moon. Think about the abundance that has manifested in your life and feel it overflow out of you. Begin to trace a line with your activator over the top branch of crystals. Do this by starting above the moonstone, moving it to selenite and back to center. Moving in a clockwise motion, repeat this process on the next line of crystals. Continue this motion five times around the entire grid. As you do this, envision a sparkling white light that descends from the glowing full moon in the sky and down to your altar. Repeat these words:

> Moonlight, so bright, on this dark night,
> Descend from up above and enter this space with your glowing love.
> Crystals filled with lunar essence combine your energy
> And let magic flow abundantly!

5. Visualize how the lunar light saturates your space with harmony. Once this is done, your grid is activated. Give thanks to the crystals and the moon. Move forward in perfect love and perfect trust, knowing that you are a magnet for abundance.

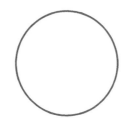

Full Moon Tarot Spread

Full moons are a perfect time for divination practices, and many witches use the potency of this phase to gaze into their futures. Tarot has become abundantly popular in the last decade as more and more people look to the symbolism of the cards to interpret their destiny. Whether you are a novice reader or adept in your divine dealings, this spell involves utilizing your tarot deck for assistance in your intentions.

YOU WILL NEED:

A tarot deck

Moonstone crystal

8 double-terminated quartz or amethyst crystals

Journal

FURTHER CONSIDERATIONS:

- **Timing:** When the full moon falls on a Monday; in the planetary hour of the moon; or when the moon is in Cancer.

- **Attire:** Purple, silver, white, or skyclad.

- **Incense:** Lavender.

- **Deity:** Selene/Luna, Hekate, or Lilith.

- **Affirmation:** "I see my future with perfect vision."

PERFORMING THE SPELL:

1. Ground and center yourself by creating a sacred space.

2. Remove the moon card from your deck and place it upright on your working surface. On top of it, place your moonstone. Now place the eight double-terminated quartz points around it.

3. Shuffle the deck and clear your mind of any distractions. Focus on what is going on in your life right now. Ask the moon to show you what it is you need to know to move forward to live abundantly. Once you feel the cards have been shuffled to where they need to be, cut the deck by sorting it into three separate piles. Intuitively put it back together.

4. With your left hand, begin to draw eight cards, placing them in a circle around your moon card and crystals. Placing the cards around the circle, move in a clockwise circle to reflect the phases of the moon and position them. The cards should be on the opposite side of each crystal point. The following is an explanation of the spread for further interpretation:

- Card One—Intention—Represents the intention that you need to set.
- Card Two—Action—The action that you need to take in the real world and spiritually.
- Card Three—Decisions—Represents the obstacles that may stand in the way.
- Card Four—Specifics—Provides advice regarding how to overcome the obstacles
- Card Five—Celebration—This card showcases the overall outcome.
- Card Six—Gratitude—Advises how you should give back in service to the world once your goal is obtained.
- Card Seven—Forgiveness—Represents your emotional state and what you need to tend to internally.
- Card Eight—Release—This card showcases what sacrifice must be made in order to obtain your goal and keep it.

5. Reflect upon the images you see and journal any reflections that you have.

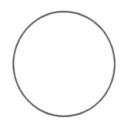

Lunar Bliss Ritual

The full moon is the peak experience of the moon cycle, and with it comes the perfect time to engage in passion, pleasure, and self-love. This ritual involves using the passion that you have for yourself as a means of raising your spiritual energy and ultimately attracting abundance into your life. It invites you to call upon the moon goddess Lilith to help you explore your passions freely and use self-love as a source of personal empowerment.

YOU WILL NEED:

Image of Lilith

Red candle

Sensuality Oil (equal parts rose, hibiscus, and patchouli with a drop of cinnamon)

Red rose

Hand mirror

Garnet crystal

Glass of your favorite libation

FURTHER CONSIDERATIONS:

- **Timing:** When the full moon falls on a Monday, Tuesday, or Friday; in the planetary hour of the moon, Mars, or Venus; or when the moon is in Scorpio.

- **Attire:** Red satin robes, lingerie, or skyclad.

- **Incense:** Dragon's blood, musk, or rose.

- **Deity:** Lilith.

- **Affirmation:** "I am empowered in bliss."

1. Begin by constructing a small altar to Lilith on your nightstand using the materials listed. This will act as the focal point of the ritual and help align her energies with your intention. You will not only be worshipping Lilith in this moment; you will be worshipping yourself through her.

2. Before you begin, take a bath or hot shower. Dress yourself in any lotions or oils afterward that help get you in the mood. Also, dress the candle with the Sensuality Oil.

3. Slip into your bed. Light your candle and raise your glass to Lilith. Repeat these words:

> By *the power of fire, Lilith I admire.*
> With *your dark beauty and grace, I welcome you into this space.*
> I *raise this glass to you, Lilith, and with this sip I welcome you to me,*
> *Your primal power and energy.*

4. Take a sip of your libation. Close your eyes and visualize the dark glamour of Lilith filling your body in a rich, red haze. Take hold of your hand mirror and look deep within your eyes. Say something to the effect of:

> Lilith, *temptress, seductress, and goddess,*
> I *see you through me, igniting my sensuality.*

5. Place the mirror on your nightstand, positioning it so that it reflects onto you. Mirrors are said to be portals to Lilith's cave and act as a gateway for her in magical practices. Focus on your goals, your ambitions, and intentions that you have been setting. Visualize them coming true and offer this experience to Lilith as an act of gratitude.

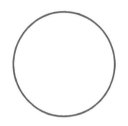

Lunar Rejuvenation Spell

This is a simple self-care spell to recharge and regroup by the light of the full moon.

YOU WILL NEED:

White candles (optional)

2 teaspoons Epsom salts

3 drops gardenia or jasmine oil

Moonstone crystal

Pillow

FURTHER CONSIDERATIONS:

- **Timing:** This spell can be performed on any day and at any time so long as the moon is full.

- **Attire:** White or skyclad.

- **Incense:** Gardenia or lavender.

- **Deity:** Selene/Luna.

- **Music:** Play soft, soothing music or binary beats to stimulate restful sleep in the background.

- **Affirmation:** "I am recharged and potent."

PERFORMING THE SPELL:

1. Begin by taking a bath illuminated with white candles. Add the Epsom salts and oil and relax in the warm water. Think about all that you have been doing and how, right now in this moment, you are one with yourself and the power of the moon.

2. Once your bath is complete, dry off and arrange a space so that you sleep directly in front of a window that gets light from the full moon. Holding the moonstone in your hands, say:

> *Soothe my sleep so that I can once again be at full peak.*

3. As you go to bed, look out at the moon and call her into your space. Ask that she help in your regrouping efforts. Say:

> *By full lunar light,*
> *I rest my head and say good night,*
> *To recharge, regroup, and rest*
> *So that I can be at my best.*

4. Place the moonstone under your pillow and drift off to sleep.

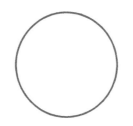

Psychic Sight Spray

To help enhance your mind's eye with psychic power, you can witch-craft the following spray for whenever you are conducting divination practices such as tarot reading or scrying. This recipe has been tailored after my dear friend and witchy sister Tonya Brown's personal recipe.

YOU WILL NEED:

4-ounce clear spray bottle

2½ ounces distilled water

¼ ounce alcohol

10 drops jasmine oil
(for moon power)

10 drops lavender oil
(for mental focus)

5 drops lemon oil
(for spirituality)

Pinch dried mugwort
(for vision)

Tumbled moonstone
(for intuition)

Silver mica (for a little
sparkle; optional)

FURTHER CONSIDERATIONS:

- **Timing:** When the full moon falls on a Monday; in the planetary hour of the moon; or when the moon is in Cancer or Pisces.

- **Attire:** Black, purple, or silver.

- **Incense:** Frankincense, jasmine, or gardenia.

- **Deity:** Selene/Luna, Hekate, or Lilith.

- **Affirmation:** "I conjure the psychic power of the moon."

1. Combine all the ingredients in the spray bottle. As you do this, tell each ingredient what its objective is, based on the notes in the materials list.

2. Seal the bottle and hold it to the sky so that you can see the moon through it. Gazing at the moon through the bottle, enchant your concoction by reciting the following charm:

> By *lunar light, enchant this spray with psychic sight.*

3. Shake the bottle vigorously. Leave it to sit in the full moon's light for the night. Use it for any divinatory purpose.

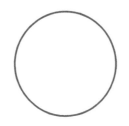

Self-Love Celebration

Who doesn't love a good excuse to eat a cupcake? This is a fun little self-love spell for you to do when you want to celebrate your best self.

YOU WILL NEED:

1 cupcake

White paper

Silver pen

Silver birthday candle

Fireproof bowl

FURTHER CONSIDERATIONS:

- **Timing:** When the full moon falls on a Friday or Sunday; in the planetary hour of Venus or the sun; or when the moon is in Taurus, Leo, or Libra.

- **Attire:** Your favorite outfit.

- **Incense:** Dragon's blood, jasmine, or rose.

- **Deity:** Aphrodite/Venus or Selene/Luna.

- **Music:** Play your favorite music.

- **Affirmation:** "I love myself. I am amazing."

PERFORMING THE RITUAL:

1. Select your favorite cupcake or make a batch from scratch.

2. At your altar, write yourself a love letter with the silver pen, expressing how amazing you are. Reflect upon your accomplishments and talents. When complete, fold the letter in thirds. Place

the cupcake in the center of your altar with the silver candle in it. Light it and say:

Silver and sweet, this tasty treat
Is a celebration of my self-worth and love,
Glowing brightly like the full moon above.

3. Set your letter on fire and let it burn down in a fireproof bowl. Let the candle burn out and then eat the cupcake, collecting a few of the crumbs.

4. Sprinkle the crumbs and ash onto the ground outside in a heart shape as a declaration of self-love and an offering to the moon.

CHAPTER 8

Waning Gibbous Moon: *Express Gratitude*

After the peak of the moon's growing power, it begins the journey back to new. The entire waning half of the moon cycle is traditionally thought to be a period of release; however, this can be refined by each specific phase. The waning gibbous moon is directly after the moon's maturation and lasts for a period of seven days. After harvesting and manifesting your intentions during the previous cycles, this is now the perfect time to offer thanks for the abundance in your life.

POTION

SPELLS/RITUALS/CEREMONIES

Giving Thanks for Abundance

Gratitude is one of the major parts of successful spellcasting. Rituals of gratitude ultimately attract more abundance into your life, helping you become a magnet for achieving all of your heart's desires. Furthermore, you remain in a more positive mind-set when you focus on the reasons to be grateful in life. Take a moment to jot down a few things that you are grateful for in your life and the results of the magic you are making. For instance, "I am grateful for my clean bill of health," "I am grateful for the obstacles that I have overcome," or "I am grateful to have removed myself from that which is holding me back."

_____

_____

_____

_____

_____

The series of spells that follow are all rituals of gratitude that you can incorporate into your moon magic during the waning gibbous phase of the moon.

Moon Matcha

Green tea has been consumed during many rituals for spiritual purposes throughout the world. Matcha is a special variety of green tea leaves that have been ground into an ultrafine powder. Both green tea leaves and roses have metaphysical properties that correspond with spiritual harmony. Likewise, green and pink are both colors for the heart chakra—and this potion assists in opening it up to express gratitude for the abundance within your life.

YOU WILL NEED:

Ice

Cocktail shaker

½ cup milk (I recommend almond)

5 tablespoons rosewater

½ cup water

1 teaspoon matcha tea powder

Pinch edible rose petals

FURTHER CONSIDERATIONS

- **Instead of using store-bought rosewater or simple syrup, make your own! See page 120.**

PREPARING THE POTION:

1. Add ice to your cup of choice.

2. In a cocktail shaker, add the milk and rosewater. Shake vigorously while you think about all that you have to be grateful for in life. Pour over the ice.

3. Rinse out the shaker.

4. Add the water and matcha powder to the shaker and shake vigorously. Matcha powder has a hard time dissolving in water, so you will need to be very forceful with your shaking to ensure there are no clumps of powder. One way to do this is to not add the full amount all at once and to instead gradually add it in.

5. Pour the matcha water into the cup with the ice and rose milk. Sprinkle rose petals on top to your liking and enjoy.

Creating an Ancestral Altar

A common practice that many witches and other practitioners of the magical community engage in involves connecting with and honoring ancestors. Every one of us has an ancestry and lineage of individuals who have come before us. By honoring them, we begin to tap into our spiritual heritage and acknowledge the meaning of their lives. The following practice involves creating an ancestral altar. Do not be discouraged if you do not know your ancestry. You can always honor the unknown and forgotten blood ancestors, dear friends who have passed, or even the spirits of the land.

YOU WILL NEED:

Photos of family members who have departed. Note that these photos should not include any living individuals.

White seven-day candle

Glass of water

Coins or other money

Human indulgences (flowers, cigarettes, cigars, wine, liquor, food, etc. Be creative!)

FURTHER CONSIDERATIONS:

- **Timing:** Any time during the waning gibbous moon and honored on a continual basis.

- **Attire:** White.

- **Incense:** Copal or sandalwood.

- **Deity:** Hekate.

- **Affirmation:** "I honor my ancestors."

1. Determine the ancestors you wish to honor and gather an arrangement of items that represent the spirits you are seeking to engage with. If this is family, collect photos of the departed, trinkets passed down to you in their parting, and/or items they enjoyed in life.

2. Dedicate a space for your ancestral altar and regularly tend to it. Keeping a strong connection to your familiar spirits will keep your connection to the other side stronger and safer.

3. Place the white candle in the center of your altar. Arrange your photos and remaining offerings around the space as you see fit. You will want to make sure you have at least one glass filled with fresh water at all times for them. This should be refreshed daily and is a small token of gratitude to the dead. They also are partial to money, particularly coin offerings, and any vices that they may have had, such as a bottle of wine or other alcohol or a pack of cigarettes.

4. After your altar has been created, light the white candle and call to your ancestors. Let them know of your love for them and that they have not been forgotten. Ask them to come and sit on the altar and tell them it is a place for you to honor them.

5. Next, make a meal that represents something they would have liked to eat. Place some of it on the altar while you eat the rest in front of them. Leave the food for them to enjoy until it starts to go bad, then discard.

6. Make an effort each day to spend time with the ancestors, not just when you need something from them. These are spirits who are always around and who care and have love for you. Share any big news, excitement, or concerns with them.

Embracing Obstacles

All obstacles present new experiences for us to learn and grow from. It is through embracing these hardships that we learn just how strong we are.

YOU WILL NEED:

Knife or toothpick

White candle in your identified gender

Lemon oil

Round casserole dish or fireproof plate

1 tablespoon dried lemon peel

1 tablespoon dried mint

1 teaspoon rock salt

FURTHER CONSIDERATIONS:

- **Timing:** When the waning gibbous moon falls on a Saturday; in the planetary hour of Saturn; or when the moon is in Scorpio or Capricorn.

- **Attire:** Black and white.

- **Incense:** Copal or sandalwood.

- **Deity:** Lilith.

- **Affirmation:** "I embrace life's challenges."

PERFORMING THE SPELL:

1. Carve your name into the figurine candle with a knife or toothpick. Dress the candle with lemon oil and place it in the center of your casserole dish or fireproof plate.

2. Mix the dried herbs and salt together evenly into a blend. Create a ring around the candle using the mixture.

3. Light the candle and say:

> By the light of this candle, may my gratitude glow
> As I give thanks to life's challenges, for they present an opportunity to grow.
> Through these obstacles, an inner strength will start to show
> And my personal power will begin to flow.

4. Reflect upon the challenges and obstacles that are presenting themselves to you right now and the opportunity for learning that they provide as the candle burns.

Honoring Anger

Honoring anger honors yourself. It tells the universe "I deserve better!" Not only does it help you set healthy boundaries, but it also lets the universe know just what you *don't* want so that you can focus on what you do want.

YOU WILL NEED:

Your favorite angry music

Elderflower oil

Red candle

FURTHER CONSIDERATIONS:

- **Timing:** When the waning gibbous moon falls on a Tuesday or Saturday; in the planetary hour of Mars or Saturn; or when the moon is in Aries, Scorpio, or Capricorn.

- **Attire:** Black.

- **Incense:** Dragon's blood.

- **Deity:** Hekate or Lilith.

- **Affirmation:** "I am thankful for my anger."

PERFORMING THE SPELL:

1. Play music that elicits anger in you, something powerful that gets you into the right state of mind.

2. Anoint your forehead, throat, heart, and the candle with elderflower oil. Light the candle and start to think about all the things that make you angry: past relationships, injustice, etc.

3. Focus intently on the anger within. Say:

> On this night, in this hour, I call upon the anger in me.
> May it rise and be set free.

4. Unleash the most primal scream into the candle.

5. When you're finished, gaze into your candle and state:

> As this flame burns, I honor my anger and ask that the rage in me
> Be transformed into healthy boundaries.

6. Let the candle burn out and bury any remains under the light of the waning moon.

Honoring a Relationship/Friendship

We all need love. Experiencing a close and intimate partnership with anyone can be an amazing experience. It does not have to be only romantic, either. Forging friendships or bonding with family members establishes intimacy while squashing feelings of loneliness. This next spell can be used for romantic relationships, friendships, or family. It is designed to tell the universe how thankful you are for the person or people in your life who provide you with security, strength, and love.

YOU WILL NEED:

Framed photo of the individual(s) you are honoring

Large bowl

1 cup spring water

Pink seven-day candle

Gardenia oil

Loose mother of pearl (1 for each person you are celebrating and 1 for you; super easy to obtain on Etsy)

Pink rose

Pink pouch

FURTHER CONSIDERATIONS:

- **Timing:** The first day of the waning gibbous moon; in the planetary hour of Venus; or when the moon is in Taurus or Libra.

- **Attire:** Pink.

- **Incense:** Rose.

- **Deity:** Aphrodite/Venus, Selene/Luna, or Yemaya.

- **Affirmation:** "I am thankful for [name of individual(s)]."

PERFORMING THE SPELL:

1. Set up a framed photo of you and the individual(s) you are honoring. In front of that, place the bowl. Fill the bowl with water.

2. Place the candle in the center of the bowl. Anoint it with the gardenia oil.

3. Light the wick and say:

> By *the light of this flame, I celebrate the relationship/friendship*
> I *have with* [name of individual(s)].

4. Pick up one of the pearls and say:

> *May you represent the gratitude in me.*

Toss the pearl into the water. Now pick up the next pearl and say:

> *May you represent the purity of* [name of individual].

Repeat the last part for any remaining individuals.

5. Pick up the rose and, one by one, remove the petals and drop them into the bowl. Reflect upon the relationship/friendship that you have. Think about all of the amazing memories that you share and how happy you are for having this person in your life. As you pick off the petals, say:

> *Rose, full of beauty and grace, represent my gratitude and love.*

6. Now gaze into the flame and recite the following:

> I *am thankful for my relationship/friendship with* [name of individual].
> As *this candle burns, may it represent my gratitude.*

7. Let the candle burn as you further reflect upon the memories you share and visualize the memories you wish to make in the future. Extinguish the candle and return to light it each subsequent night during the waning gibbous phase of the moon. By the seventh day, the water should have evaporated and the petals started to dry. Once this has occurred, place the pearls and dried petals into the pink pouch and leave it in front of the frame. Anoint the bag with the gardenia oil and relight the candle (if any wax remains) for each subsequent waning gibbous phase until it has been completely diminished.

Lunar Thanksgiving Ritual

This is an extensive ritual of gratitude to celebrate abundance in your life.

YOU WILL NEED:

White candles

Lemon oil

Lavender oil

Epsom salts

Glass

Roses

Piece of white paper

Pen

Piece of black paper

Cauldron or fireproof pot

FURTHER CONSIDERATIONS:

- **Timing:** Any time during the waning gibbous phase of the moon.

- **Attire:** White or silver.

- **Incense:** Jasmine, lavender, or sandalwood.

- **Deity:** Any.

- **Affirmation:** "I give thanks for abundance in my life."

PERFORMING THE SPELL:

1. Prior to your ritual, take a bath. Light white candles within the bathroom and add a mixture of lemon and lavender oils to the waters with some Epsom salts to cleanse yourself. Before leaving the bath, gather some of the bathwater in a glass.

2. Enter your ritual space and decorate your altar with the roses. Cast a full circle as outlined in chapter 2 (see page 23). Light the white candle and state:

This ritual is dedicated to express my gratitude.
By the light of this flame, as the moon begins to wane,
I am thankful for my abundance that has since came.

3. Give thanks to any deity, spirit, or ancestor you wish for the abundance you have received.

4. On the piece of white paper, write a list of the things that have brought abundance in your life. On the piece of black paper, write a list of the hardships you've endured that have made you stronger.

5. Touch the corner of the white paper to the flame and drop it into the cauldron or pot while saying:

Accept this petition as my thanks for the blessings
of abundance I have received.
May the element of fire transform my thankfulness so that it can
be carried away by air.

6. Watch the paper burn, then repeat step 5 with the black paper, saying:

Accept this petition as my thanks for the hardships I have endured.
May the element of fire transform my thankfulness so that it can be carried
away by air.

7. Sit and reflect upon your gratitude. Once finished, add the bathwater to the ashes in the cauldron or pot. Say:

By the power of water and the emotional current in me, I offer my gratitude.

8. Take one of the roses and remove the petals, placing them into the cauldron as well. Say:

By the power of earth, the foundation of abundance, I offer my gratitude.

9. Close the ritual and take the pot outside. Pour the concoction on the earth and declare:

Moon, please accept this offering of gratitude for contributing
to the abundance in my life!

Minimalism Moon Spell

We live in a materialistic world where success is often attributed to how much we have. However, this materialism often comes with wastefulness. This spell is designed to get you thinking about what you really need and calls upon you to be grateful for what you have. Instead of spring cleaning . . . we are lunar cleaning.

YOU WILL NEED:

White candle

Vanilla oil

Any items of yours that you no longer feel are necessary to own

Bags or boxes

FURTHER CONSIDERATIONS:

- **Timing:** When the waning gibbous moon falls on a Saturday; in the planetary hour of Saturn; or when the moon is in Scorpio or Capricorn.

- **Attire:** Black or white.

- **Incense:** Sage or frankincense.

- **Affirmation:** "I minimize my possessions and am grateful for what I have."

PERFORMING THE SPELL:

1. Once night falls, anoint the white candle with the vanilla oil. Light the candle and say:

> *I am thankful for what I have, I am thankful for what I need.*
> *Let me release that which is unnecessary, and give back to those in need.*

2. Begin to go through your home and collect items that you are no longer connected to. Feel empowered in your choices of letting go and feel gratitude for what the objects have provided to you.

3. Gather all of the items and place them in the bags or boxes. As you tie the bags shut or place the lids on the boxes, bid your items farewell and know that as you release these material objects, you are being of service to others in need while making room for the universe to bring you more abundance.

4. Donate your items to a friend in need or to a homeless shelter, secondhand store, or similar establishment.

Pay It Forward Spell

Giving back is a powerful source for accumulating abundance. Here, you will literally pay it forward to someone in need with a random act of generosity.

YOU WILL NEED:

Clear glass wine bottle   Paper

Pyrite crystal   Pen

Monetary donation   Cord

FURTHER CONSIDERATIONS:

- **Timing:** Any time during the waning gibbous moon.

- **Attire:** Green, silver, or gold.

- **Incense:** Lavender or mint.

- **Deity:** Artemis/Diana, Nanna/Sin, or Yemaya.

- **Affirmation:** "I give thanks to the universe and the magic of the moon for the abundance in my life."

PERFORMING THE SPELL:

1. Take the bottle and fill it with the crystal and the money. As you add these items, think about how grateful you are to have received the money and how it will be of value to those in need.

2. On the paper, write a message to the unknown recipient. It can be something along the lines of:

Hello,
My name is [Name] and I hope you accept this offering of abundance and use it as you see fit. If you do not need it, perhaps you will add to it and pass it along to whoever is meant to receive the riches.
Blessed be,
[Name]

3. Place the cord on the bottle and bring it to your window so that it may absorb the lunar light. Say:

> *By the light of the waning moon, I give a part of me to those in need.*

4. Leave the bottle overnight, and in the morning take it to a roadside or leave it on the doorstep of a random house or establishment.

Thanking the Earth

Get ready—we are going on a field trip. To honor and give thanks to the earth, we have to plant ourselves in the great outdoors and go on a bit of a scavenger hunt. Magical foraging involves looking for herbs and other items to use in spells and rituals. Getting out into the great wild and collecting items that find you along the way will develop your intuitive awareness of the earth around you. If you live in a concrete jungle like New York, Chicago, or another major city, you can still do this, as your landscape provides a unique array of other objects that can be used. Most importantly, have fun with this. While it would make sense to do this type of ritual at night, it is much safer to do your foraging during the day. Remember to act practically with your magic!

YOU WILL NEED:

Backpack
Collection of natural items found on the hike

Incense stick in your favorite scent

FURTHER CONSIDERATIONS:

- **Timing:** When the waning gibbous moon is on a Saturday; in the planetary hour of Saturn; or when the moon is in Scorpio or Capricorn.

- **Attire:** Anything that is comfortable.

- **Affirmation:** "I honor the land in which I walk, the earth, my home."

1. In the afternoon, go into nature somewhere and intuitively allow yourself to find objects that fascinate you. These might be sticks, flowers, rocks, or other things. As you collect your items, bond with them by reflecting on their inherent magic.

2. At dusk, go to a natural body of water and erect an intricate design with the items. (This could be a creek, river, lake, ocean, or any other type of water system you can safely access.) Here you are ultimately creating a natural shrine in dedication to the earth. Arrange your collected items in a way that expresses your appreciation of the earth.

3. Light the incense stick and trace a pentagram into the air above your shrine. Kneel before the shrine and plant your hands firmly on the earth, feeling its power. Repeat the following words:

> *With the setting sun, night will come,*
> *and the moon's magic will have soon begun.*
> *I give thanks to the earth, my planet and home,*
> *And all of the natural magic which I am shown.*
> *All full of love, beauty, and grace,*
> *I honor the land, this sacred space.*

4. In this moment, meditate on the marvel of the earth. When you feel that you are finished, leave the space. Feel free to continue to frequent the space and leave earthy offerings you are drawn to while continuously honoring the beauty of the earth.

CHAPTER 9

Third Quarter Moon: *Forgive*

The third quarter is the midpoint of the entire waning phase of the moon. Another phase when the moon's illumination is completely split in half, this is a potent time to work on healing our emotional wounds with forgiveness. The art of forgiveness is a critical step to bring more abundance into our lives, because it is a catalyst for personal growth and happiness. Just like the first quarter, this is a short phase lasting for only one day. However, you can still utilize its energy the day before and after the exact phase.

POTION

SPELLS/RITUALS/CEREMONIES

Moving Forward with Forgiveness

On the following lines, record what you want to forgive in yourself and others, as well as the forgiveness you may be seeking *from* others. Some examples might be, "I forgive my failures and use them as a learning opportunity," "I forgive the person who has wronged me and have compassion for the pain they must be in to have done this to me," and "I seek forgiveness from [XYZ]." You can try to connect to the intentions you set in chapter 3 or deviate from them, as forgiveness ultimately allows you to attract more abundance on a grand scale.

_____

_____

_____

_____

_____

Forgiveness is the first step in the more focused and intense releasing and letting go that is practiced in the next phase of the moon (waning crescent). If you feel inclined, use the following spells to facilitate forgiveness at this time.

Cham-Pain Potion

Forgiveness comes with pain. In fact, the act of forgiveness can be painful, but it is ultimately sugary sweet because it heals the heart. This "cham-pain" potion calls on the protective qualities of elderflower and lemon with the festivity of champagne to help soothe your emotions. The potion can be enjoyed on its own or added to any of the spells and rituals that follow.

YOU WILL NEED:

Champagne flute

½ ounce elderflower liquor

½ ounce fresh lemon juice

3 to 4 ounces chilled champagne, prosecco, or cava

Lemon twist (optional)

Fresh strawberry (optional)

FURTHER CONSIDERATIONS:

- For a mocktail version, substitute an iced white tea blend, elderflower simple syrup, and lemonade.

- Make your own elderflower syrup by combining 1 cup of water, 1 cup of sugar, and ½ cup of culinary elderflowers in a saucepan. Bring to a boil and then simmer for about 10 minutes until thick. Strain into an airtight container, removing any residual floral bits, and store in the refrigerator to cool and keep fresh.

PREPARING THE POTION:

1. Chill a tall champagne flute.

2. Add the elderflower liquor and lemon juice.

3. Top off with champagne.

4. Add a lemon twist or strawberry for decoration if you feel up for it.

5. Sit and savor in front of your lunar altar while you contemplate forgiveness and what it means. Whom do you forgive, and what circumstances are you willing to move past and let go of? Reflect on these and allow yourself to heal.

Embracing Vulnerability

Many people avoid being vulnerable for fear that doing so will cause emotional turmoil. However, vulnerability is the glue to all of our other emotions. Here is a simple bath spell that calls on the emotional, vulnerable essence of water.

YOU WILL NEED:

Lavender oil

Rosemary oil

3 dark blue candles (any size)

3 light blue candles (any size)

1 white candle (any size)

Tumbled amethyst

Dark blue bath bomb

FURTHER CONSIDERATIONS:

- **Timing:** When the third quarter falls on a Monday; in the planetary hour of the moon; or when the moon is in Cancer or Pisces.

- **Attire:** Skyclad.

- **Incense:** Lavender.

- **Deity:** Yemaya.

- **Affirmation:** "I embrace vulnerability."

PERFORMING THE SPELL:

1. Add a drop of each oil to the candles and position them around the bathtub.

2. Draw a warm bath. Add three drops of each oil and the amethyst crystal to the water. Light the candles and extinguish electric light from the space.

3. Drop the bath bomb into the water and enter the bath. Watch the bath bomb fizz and swirl around, turning your water a rich blue hue. Close your eyes, ground and center yourself, and call upon the moon and tides:

As the moon affects the tides,
My emotional guard shall now subside.
I allow myself to embrace vulnerability
imparted by the waters surrounding me.

4. Enjoy the remainder of your bath and reflect upon the joys that can be had from being more vulnerable, open, and loving. When finished, let the water drain from the tub while you stay in it. Once the tub is empty, say, "I forgive myself and embrace vulnerability."

Forgive Failure

Here we will suspend negative self-talk and forgive ourselves for failure so we can move forward.

YOU WILL NEED:

Mirror

Small bowl that will hold all materials

Spring water

Pinch of salt

Pinch of sugar

Light blue votive candle

Pearl or tumbled rhodonite

FURTHER CONSIDERATIONS:

- **Timing:** When the third quarter is on a Monday; in the planetary hour of the moon; or when the moon is in Cancer.

- **Attire:** White, blue, or pink.

- **Incense:** Jasmine.

- **Deity:** Artemis/Diana, Aphrodite/Venus, or Yemaya.

- **Affirmation:** "I have forgiven my failures."

PERFORMING THE SPELL:

1. Determine a mirror you can use for the spell. This can easily be done with a mirror in a private bathroom, with a hand mirror, or with a compact.

2. Fill the bowl with the water. Add the salt and sugar. Using the index finger of your dominant hand, stir the water counterclockwise three times.

3. Place the candle into the water and add the pearl or crystal. Light the candle, saying:

> By salt and sugar, by water and fire,
> Opposition fueled with desire to transpire.
> I release failure and see it as success.
> Personal growth coming, I am truly blessed.

4. Take some of the water on your finger and rub it onto the mirror in front of you, making counterclockwise circles in the reflection. Gaze deep into your eyes and say:

> My failures are blessings in disguise.

5. Blow out the candle and save it to repeat anytime you are feeling bogged down by feelings of failure.

Forgive Someone Who Has Wronged You

When someone hurts you, they are usually hurting themselves. As upsetting as it is to be wronged, it is important to have compassion for them. Here is a spell that allows you to release the heaviness of your pain and embrace the lightness of forgiveness.

YOU WILL NEED:

Dark rock   White feather

FURTHER CONSIDERATIONS:

- **Timing:** When the third quarter is on a Monday; in the planetary hour of the moon; or when the moon is in Cancer.

- **Attire:** Black and white.

- **Incense:** Lavender or rose.

- **Deity:** Artemis/Diana or Yemaya.

- **Affirmation:** "I humbly forgive [name of the person]."

PERFORMING THE SPELL:

1. Outside, under the light of the moon, holding the rock in your right hand and the feather in your left, close your eyes and say:

Light as a feather and hard as a rock,
I intend to forgive [name of the person] *for the wrong that was brought.*

2. Hold your right hand with the rock out in front of you. Channel all of your negative emotions for the situation into the rock. Throw the rock and say:

I let go of the heaviness in my heart.

3. Hold your left hand with the feather out in front of you. Visualize yourself and the person who wronged you together. Focus on the happy times and memories you've shared and how you wish to do so again in the future. Say:

> By the grace and lightness of this feather,
> I forgive thee so we can move forward together.

4. Blow the feather to the wind. Connect with that person soon after with a forgiving mind to wipe the slate clean.

Lunar Liberation Spell

Do you ever just feel the need to cut yourself free? So often we can get caught up with negativity and feelings of imprisonment bestowed upon us by our circumstances. This is toxic when it comes to creating abundance in your life, as negative thoughts and patterns limit your ability to reach success. This spell offers forgiveness and freedom from self-imposed restriction.

YOU WILL NEED:

White candlestick

Knife or toothpick

4 thin black cords

4 obsidian obelisks (at least 2 inches in height)

Pizza pan

Eight of swords tarot card

Garnet crystal

Rosemary oil

FURTHER CONSIDERATIONS:

- **Timing:** When the third quarter is on a Tuesday or Saturday; in the planetary hour of Mars or Saturn; or when the moon is in Aries, Scorpio, or Capricorn.

- **Attire:** Black.

- **Incense:** Dragon's blood.

- **Deity:** Artemis/Diana or Lilith.

- **Affirmation:** "I liberate myself from limitation."

PERFORMING THE SPELL:

1. The white candle is going to be a representation of you and the peace you are trying to create through your liberation. Carve your name into the wax of the candle. Add any bio-bits to the carvings,

such as your saliva, hair, nail clippings, or blood, to connect the candle to you.

2. Tie a black cord to each of the obsidian obelisks. Make sure that the strings are equal in length. Tie the loose end of each string to the candle.

3. Place the candle in the center of the pizza pan, with the obelisks in the positions of the four cardinal directions. Make sure the string is taut.

4. Between you and the items, position the eight of swords card. The eight of swords is known to represent self-imprisonment and mental challenges that come from fear. The powerful symbolism of the card can provide the liberation you need. On top of the card, place the garnet crystal—known for providing personal power and strength.

5. Drizzle the candle with rosemary oil and repeat the following incantation:

Moon, hear my call, hear my plea.
I ask that you help set me free!
Break the chains and provide escape
So that I may move forward with a new future to shape!

6. Watch the candle burn down. Eventually it will make its way to the cords. They will either drop freely or catch fire and detach from the candle. When this happens, slam your palms together hard to make a huge clap. Staring at the flame, say:

It is done, and the spell has begun. I am free, so mote it be.

7. Remain with the candle until it has completely burned out, meditating on your newfound freedom.

8. Move forward knowing that you are free from the limitations you create. The next time you are feeling trapped, sit in the center of your obelisks and meditate on the eight of swords card.

Justice Spell

Justice is an aspect of forgiveness because it provides the closure necessary to move on. Life, and witchcraft for that matter, is not all love and light. There is a darkness that comes with it, just like the moon. This justice spell can be performed for someone who has wronged you as a form of release or as an act of social justice on a larger scale. While bragging and posting about your spells in general does no good and is highly discouraged, it is even more important to not let on about the justice work that you are doing, as the recipient may catch wind of it and enact their own type of protection against it.

YOU WILL NEED:

Photo of adversary

1 High John root

Justice tarot card

Judgment tarot card

2 orange candles with holders

Knife or toothpick

Purple candle

3 drops rosemary oil

3 drops black pepper oil

Black tape

FURTHER CONSIDERATIONS:

- **Timing:** When the third quarter falls on a Saturday; in the planetary hour of Saturn; or when the moon is in Libra.

- **Attire:** Purple, orange, or black.

- **Incense:** Frankincense.

- **Deity:** Hekate.

- **Affirmation:** "I seek justice for [XYZ]."

1. Place the photo of your adversary in the center of your altar space with the High John root on top of it. Place the justice tarot card horizontally on the right side of the photo with the top of the card pointed outward. Position the judgment card on the left side of the photo with the top of the card pointed outward.

2. Add the orange candles behind the other objects at an equal distance apart.

3. Carve the planetary symbol for Saturn on the purple candle. Add three drops each of the rosemary and black pepper oils to the carving and rub them into the wax. Place the candle directly behind the photo of the person. Light the wick and say:

> *In order to absolve my mind, justice must be involved at this time.*
> *All powers of the universe, I call on thee, and the waning moon split in half equally.*
> *On this night and upon this very hour, may karma have full power.*

4. Now pick up the purple candle and tilt it so that wax falls on the face of the individual. Reposition the candle above the photo.

5. Place each hand upon the tarot cards and say:

> *May the powers of justice and judgment arise and fall side by side.*
> *I seek your assistance in righting the wrong of* [speak the situation out loud]
> *As executed by* [name of person/people responsible].

6. Now hold the photo with the High John root and begin wrapping the black tape around the two items to further bind the person from creating any more negativity or havoc. As you do this, state:

> *I bind* [name].

7. Place the taped photo back in the center. Keep the items stationed and return to them daily during the planetary hour of Saturn. Relight the candles then and re-perform the spell until the candle has been spent.

Queen of Cups Compassion Spell

This is another tarot spell that calls upon compassion when facing guilt.

YOU WILL NEED:

Queen of cups tarot card

Small cup or cordial glass

White or pink rose

Spring water

Tumbled rose quartz

Crown charm

Light pink or blue
drawstring bag

FURTHER CONSIDERATIONS:

- **Timing:** When the third quarter is on a Monday; in the planetary hour of the moon; or when the moon is in Cancer.

- **Attire:** White, blue, or pink.

- **Incense:** Jasmine.

- **Deity:** Artemis/Diana, Aphrodite/Venus, or Yemaya.

- **Affirmation:** "I have self-compassion."

PERFORMING THE SPELL:

1. Position the queen of cups card so that it stands and faces you on your altar. Place the cup in front of it.

2. Remove the petals from the rose and use them to make a heart shape around the cup and card. In this moment, have empathy for yourself and the hardships or situations that cause you feelings of guilt.

3. Fill the cup with spring water. Add the rose quartz and crown charm to the water.

4. Close your eyes and call forth the queen of compassion:

> *I call forth the queen of cups and offer my guilt for grace.*
> *It is compassion that I wish to embrace.*

5. Look deeply at your queen of cups card and reflect upon compassion.

6. Leave the materials on your altar until the water has evaporated and the petals have dried. Place the crystal, charm, and dried petals into the drawstring bag. Carry the bag or hold on to it when you need to call upon the queen's compassion.

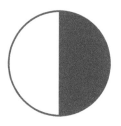

Shadow Self Pathworking

Our shadow self refers to the part of us that is dark, neglected, and taboo to the society around us. It is filled with rage, pain, and other qualities that are dark and twisty. The shadow's traits are sometimes thought of as being a dark unconscious current that runs through us. Sometimes people think it is best to repress the shadow and hold it at bay, but it is important to connect to it. After all, even the moon has a period of total darkness, for it allows rebirth and understanding.

YOU WILL NEED:

Black candle

Mugwort oil

Dried rosemary

Black moonstone

FURTHER CONSIDERATIONS:

- **Timing: Any night during the third quarter.**

- **Attire: Black.**

- **Incense: Frankincense, sandalwood, or copal.**

- **Deity: Hekate or Lilith.**

- **Affirmation: "I merge with my shadow."**

PERFORMING THE SPELL:

1. Anoint your candle with mugwort oil and roll it in dried rosemary.

2. Place the candle on your altar and light it. Extinguish all other light sources in your room so that you remain in total darkness with the exception of the candlelight.

3. Holding the black moonstone in your palms, position yourself in a comfortable pose for meditation. You may wish to sit in lotus pose on a floor pillow, lie back on a yoga mat, or sit comfortably in a chair. If you are going the chair route, be sure that your feet rest planted on the floor and do not dangle.

4. Slowly enter a meditative state. Clear your mind from distraction and focus on counting backward from 10 to 1. You may visualize the numbers in your head, playing in front of you as they would on a movie screen.

5. Visualize yourself on the shores of a black sand beach—cold and wet. You see nothing but the waning crescent moon in the distance. You follow it, walking through a vast wasteland.

6. Make note of any people, animals, or creatures you see on the way. How do you feel? Even if you are scared, it is important that you do not look back.

7. You eventually make your way to a cave. You make out serpents gathered on the rocks near the mouth. They hiss at you—what are they telling you? They move down and slither into the cave. You follow.

8. After stepping down a winding path of rocks, you make your way to the center of the cave, and there is a huge bonfire. You sit in front of it and focus on the warm light in the darkness.

9. Soon a cloaked figure moves from the shadows and greets you on the opposite side of the flame. It is your shadow self, with a message for you.

10. Remain in a trance and allow the rest of the meditation to play out accordingly. When you come back to the material world, allow yourself a moment to reground. Write down any revelations or messages you received. Offer your gratitude and close the circle.

Show Me Forgiveness Spell

Any kind of relationship can have friction. No matter how hard you try, someone is bound to get their feelings hurt at some point, whether the act was intentional or not. In these instances, use a sweetening spell to gain reconciliation. Sweetening spells are used in various folk magic practices, and this one is a take on the traditional hoodoo honey jar.

YOU WILL NEED:

Square paper

Pen

Small honey jar

2 fresh white rosebuds

1 High John root

1 pearl

Tumbled rhodonite

Tumbled rose quartz

1 vanilla bean, cut in half

White taper candle

Bowl or plate

FURTHER CONSIDERATIONS:

- **Timing:** When the third quarter is on a Monday or Friday; in the planetary hour of the moon or Venus; or when the moon is in Taurus or Libra.

- **Attire:** Pink or white.

- **Incense:** Rose or jasmine.

- **Deity:** Aphrodite/Venus or Yemaya.

- **Affirmation:** "I am sorry for my actions and seek forgiveness."

PERFORMING THE SPELL:

1. Begin by writing out a petition. To do this, write the name of the person you seek forgiveness from in the center of the paper three times while repeating the names out loud. Turn the paper so that the

name appears vertically and then write your name three times over the other name. Now, write "forgiveness" over and over in a circle around the names until they are fully enclosed. Fold the paper in half twice and set it aside.

2. Open the honey jar and eat three scoops of the honey. With each scoop, say:

Honey so sweet, show me forgiveness.

3. Push the folded petition deep into the honey jar and say:

Sticky and sweet, forgiveness I seek between me and [name of the person].

4. Now add each remaining ingredient and advise what it needs to do:

Rosebuds, bloom with forgiveness.
High John, grant luck and success.
Pearl, show mercy and grace.
Rhodonite, bestow compassion and harmony.
Rose quartz, heal emotional wounds.
Vanilla, seal forgiveness with your sweetness.

5. Place the lid on the honey jar and gently light the bottom of your white candle so that the wax is malleable. Stick it to the top of the lid.

6. Place the jar on your bowl or plate and add it to your lunar altar. Light the candle, close your eyes, and say this incantation for forgiveness:

Illuminated by the half lunar light, I seek to make things right.
[Name of the person], *may we move forward from the darkness of night.*
Forgive me, please forgive me. Show me forgiveness.

7. Let the candle burn for an hour. Relight it each day until it is extinguished, reciting the same prayer while visualizing reconciliation. If the candle burns out before you receive forgiveness, add another and continue the process. Once you and the other party have made up, bury the jar.

CHAPTER 10

Waning Crescent Moon: *Surrender and Release*

 As we come full circle, we reach our last phase of the moon. The waning crescent consists of the final seven days of the moon before it returns to new. Each day the crescent will get thinner and thinner until it is the blackness of new again. In these final days, it is a time to embrace the darker aspects of reality—the necessary death that leads to rebirth. It is a time to wipe the slate clean and ultimately surrender that which no longer serves us so that we can make room for further abundance.

POTION

SPELLS/RITUALS/CEREMONIES

Enlightened Release

It may seem scary, but this final step in practicing lunar magic and calling for abundance is arguably the most important. The art of letting go allows you to get rid of what no longer serves and rebirth your magical self with a fresh set of intentions at the start of the new moon. Use the following lines to record what it is that you wish to release and surrender at this time. Some examples might be "I release myself from the people and situations that do not serve my highest good" and "I embrace the ending of my relationship with [XYZ] and move forward on my new path."

_____

_____

_____

_____

_____

In the remaining pages, you'll find the final spell and ritual suggestions for this book. Each uniquely evokes the themes of surrender, letting go, and death. Use them as you see fit.

Surrender Sangria

Since wine goes through a fermentation process, this is a literal representation of transformation from fruit to wine. Sangria derives from Spain and is made by mixing red or white wine with fruit and other juices that add sweetness to the bold flavor of the libation. Since the waning crescent signifies death and letting go, let's use a dry red wine and sweet juices for a bit of edible alchemy representing the sweetness of letting go.

YOU WILL NEED:

1 bag frozen strawberries with syrup

Pitcher or carafe

1 bottle dry red wine

½ cup brandy

½ cup pomegranate juice

½ cup cranberry juice

Chopped grapes

Chopped oranges

Chopped lemons

Dash of cinnamon

FURTHER CONSIDERATIONS:

- For a mocktail version, remove the alcohol and add more juice of your choice.

- Since the waning moon represents the decline of the moon, this is best served cold.

- Store leftovers covered in the refrigerator.

PREPARING THE POTION:

1. Place the bag of frozen strawberries out on your counter for about an hour prior to making the sangria. You will want the syrup to be defrosted; the strawberries can remain frozen to act as ice.

2. Add the strawberries and defrosted syrup to the pitcher or carafe and pour all the liquids in.

3. Slice your selected fresh fruit and add it to the concoction.

4. Add in a bit of cinnamon to your liking and stir the liquid in a counterclockwise movement to symbolize the reversal and letting go that are necessary for surrender.

Cord Cutting Ritual

A cord cutting spell is a type of healing ritual used to cut the emotional bond between you and another. The ritual is not intended to cause hate or chaos in the other's life but rather to free yourself from the toxicity they have engulfed you with. These spells are typically done at the end of a relationship or close friendship but have also been used to release family members who dangerously cause you mental anguish.

YOU WILL NEED:

Photo of you	Black candlestick
Photo of other person	Black pepper oil
Hole punch	Dried rosemary
Black cord	Dried sage
Knife	Fireproof dish

FURTHER CONSIDERATIONS:

- **Timing:** When the waning crescent is on Saturday; in the planetary hour of Saturn; or when the moon is in Scorpio or Capricorn.

- **Attire:** Black.

- **Incense:** Copal or frankincense.

- **Deity:** Lilith.

- **Affirmation:** "I cut the ties that bind me and [name of person]."

PERFORMING THE SPELL:

1. First obtain a photo of yourself and a photo of the person you wish to let go. If you are unable to find a photo, write their name on a piece of paper.

2. Create a hole in each photo. Loop one end of the cord through each hole so that both photos are on opposite ends of the string.

3. Use the knife to carve your names along each side of the candle. Massage the carvings with the black pepper oil and rub the ground herbs into the pockets.

4. Sit in a comfortable position and light the candle. Place the fireproof dish nearby. Close your eyes and visualize that you are on a road with the person you wish to cut ties with. Look them dead in the eyes and focus all of your sadness, pain, and anger on this moment. Really allow yourself to be upset and angry. Know that you deserve better and that you no longer need this person in your life. Say to them, "I release you." Visualize yourself grabbing them by the shoulders and turning them around. Then begin to walk away from each other. Never look back.

5. Once you feel yourself removed from their presence, open your eyes and pick up the photos so that one is in each hand. Pull the string taut and hold it out in front of you. Say:

> I, [your name], *release* [their name].
> *In this moment and hour, I call upon the power of me,*
> *To cut the cord between us and be free.*
> *By the power of fire and waning moon,*
> *It is my desire to cut ties with you.*
> *You may no longer harbor negativity.*
> *Good luck on your journey alone, for I am set free!*

6. Place the center of the cord in the flame until it burns and breaks into two. Use the fireproof dish if need be to calm the flames. Place the piece of the other person in the dish; hold on to the photo of yourself and feel free.

7. Discard of both halves in different locations to further instill separation.

Dark Goddess Ritual

Much like the waxing crescent and full moon phases, now is another time to honor the divine feminine in the form of the Dark Goddess—a representation of drastic change and transformation. Often misunderstood as evil, she is no-nonsense, tough, and strong. She is wise and cunning, granting you that which you need over that which you want. She is the necessary death that leads to rebirth, much like the waning crescent on its journey back to the new phase. It is through paying homage to the Dark Goddess that we can learn the tough lessons necessary for our spiritual growth.

YOU WILL NEED:

Representation of the Dark Goddess (e.g., framed photo, statue, etc.)

Black candle

White or silver candles

Bouquet of dried roses

Chalice filled with Surrender Sangria (see page 180) or libation of choice

Journal (optional)

FURTHER CONSIDERATIONS:

- **Timing:** The night before the new moon.

- **Attire:** Black or deep red.

- **Incense:** Frankincense, sandalwood, or copal.

- **Deity:** Hekate or Lilith.

- **Affirmation:** "I celebrate the Dark Goddess in me."

1. Arrange your moon altar so that your representation of the Dark Goddess is in the center. Place the black candle to the right and the white or silver candle to the left. The flowers will go behind the Dark Goddess representation and the chalice in front of it.

2. Cast a circle and follow the ritual guidelines from chapter 2 (see page 23). Once your circle is set, it is time to invite the Dark Goddess into your space. Close your eyes and reach out your arms in a "Y" position up to the moon. Call her down into your circle, saying:

> I call upon the Dark Goddess of the moon,
> Mother of transformation who engulfs the silver moon with black embrace.
> She who is hidden in the shadows, she who is death and decay,
> The black water of creation and primordial sea of consciousness in me.
> Tonight I honor thee, oh dark queen of many names.
> As the cycle of the moon returns to new, I am reminded of your power and glory.
> I embrace the darkness and surrender to the transformative rebirth of
> your magic.

3. Bow in honor of the goddess and immediately raise a toast to her. Have a sip of the sangria or another libation of your choice. Do not finish the entire glass.

4. Sit and honor the Dark Goddess by reflecting upon that which you know is holding you back and that which must be surrendered in order for your growth. Remember to record any of your revaluations in a journal to look back on.

5. Once you feel moved to close the ritual, express your thanks to the goddess and deconstruct your magical boundaries. Let the remaining sangria stay on your altar as an offering to the Dark Goddess. As it molds over, it will symbolize her transformative powers.

Freeze Bad Habits

Freezer spells are used to stop people and situations from causing negativity in your life. They can be used when you have a trait you are trying to stop or to deter adversaries from causing chaos in your life. In order to bring in more abundance, you sometimes must freeze negativity to prevent it from spreading.

YOU WILL NEED:

Water from a natural source

Glass jar with a sealable lid

Black pepper

Sage

Black pen

Strip of black paper

Charcoal disc

FURTHER CONSIDERATIONS:

- **Timing:** When the waning crescent falls on a Saturday; in the planetary hour of Saturn; or when the moon is in Scorpio or Capricorn.

- **Attire:** Black.

- **Incense:** Sage or frankincense.

- **Deity:** Aphrodite/Venus or Yemaya.

- **Affirmation:** "I freeze [name of person causing conflict] for my freedom."

PERFORMING THE SPELL:

1. Retrieve water from a natural source, such as a lake, river, creek, rainfall, or ocean. Pour the water into the jar.

2. Grind the black pepper and sage and add them to the jar.

3. With the black pen, write the bad habits, people, or situations you wish to freeze on the strip of black paper. Add it to the jar.

4. Grind the charcoal disc so that it becomes a fine powder. Add it to the water. Cap the jar off and, using both hands, shake it vigorously as you say:

> *Habits of mine and thine*
> *That do not allow me to shine*
> *Shall now be frozen in time!*

5. Place the jar in the freezer.

Lunatic Necromancy

The waning crescent is also a powerful time to connect with loved ones who have departed. "Necromancy" is a term that is given to the conjuration of spirits for magical purposes. This ritual takes the process of establishing an ancestral altar one step further and becomes a means for you to commune with a departed loved one.

YOU WILL NEED:

Grave dirt from deceased individual

Coins

Ashes; bowl if not using ashes (optional)

Deceased's favorite meal

3 black candles with holders

Black lace fabric

Bowl

Replica of a human skull

White lilies

2 skeleton keys (easily found at craft stores)

Photos of the departed person

Red wine

1 teaspoon honey

Cup or chalice

Lavender or copal incense

FURTHER CONSIDERATIONS:

- **Timing:** When the waning crescent is on Saturday; in the planetary hour of Saturn; or when the moon is in Scorpio or Capricorn.

- **Attire:** Black.

- **Deity:** Hekate.

- **Affirmation:** "I seek communion with [name of departed spirit]."

1. Prior to the ritual, obtain dirt from the grave of the individual you are seeking to commune with. In exchange for the dirt, leave several coins behind as a token of payment to the dead. If your loved one was cremated instead of being buried, you may use the urn with their ashes in the ritual instead. Alternatively, you may use a representation of the dirt or urn (such as soil from your garden, or a beloved vase), as long as this substitution is imbued with your intentions.

2. Begin the ritual by preparing one of the deceased's favorite recipes and set places for you and them at your dinner table. Set a black candle in the center and light it. Ensure that the food does not have salt in it, as salt is a repellent for the dead.

3. Put the black lace fabric over your head so that you are veiled. You can use either your lunar or ancestral altar as your workstation for this ritual. Add the grave dirt (if using) to the bowl and put the skull on top. Place the bowl in the center of your altar with the vase of white lilies directly behind it. If you are using an urn of ashes, place that behind the skull, with flowers behind it. Make an "X" with the skeleton keys and place them directly in front of the skull. Position the remaining candles on either side of the items on the altar to illuminate the space. Add the remaining items as you see fit.

4. Add the red wine with a teaspoon of honey to the cup or chalice as an offering. Light the candles and incense.

5. Sit in front of the altar and call upon the departed to enter the skull. Remove the black lace fabric and uncross the keys to symbolize an opening of the veils and to open the path to communication. Eat in silence under the candlelight. Pay attention to the space and see what messages you get.

6. Once complete, let the spirit know that they may leave the skull, that you thank them for their time, and that you love them. Leave the food and wine on the altar for them until it has gone bad, and then discard.

Molting Spell: Shed Your Old Skin

The following spell calls upon the power of the serpent to assist in symbolically shedding your skin. Snakes are highly coveted animals in some paths of witchcraft and goddess worship. This is a great ritual that can be done during times of transformation, such as the end of the calendar year, your birthday, changes of the seasons, or other rites of passage.

YOU WILL NEED:

Snake representation (dried snakeskin, statue, photo, etc.)

4 white candles
(for new beginnings)

Knife

3 green candles (for healing)

3 black candles
(for letting go)

Pillow (optional)

Small piece of paper

Pen

Shovel

FURTHER CONSIDERATIONS:

- **Timing:** When the waning crescent falls on a Monday, Wednesday, or Saturday; in the planetary hour of Saturn; or when the moon is in Scorpio, Aquarius, or Pisces.

- **Attire:** White, green, or black.

- **Incense:** Nag champa.

- **Deity:** Lilith.

- **Music:** Record yourself speaking the meditation so you can play it back while executing this spell.

- **Affirmation:** "I shed what no longer serves."

1. Place the snake representation and one of the white candles on your altar. With the knife, carve an ouroboros (snake eating its tail) into it. Place the remaining candles in a circle around you, alternating colors, with enough space for you to comfortably lie down.

2. Take hold of your snake representation, light your white candle, and say:

> I call forth the sacred ancient serpent
> That represents life, death, and rebirth.
> Heal me and allow me to let go of my past and be reborn.
> May I shed my skin and feel comfort in the wisdom
> That I am not who I once was and will continue to change shape and form
> Physically, mentally, and spiritually.
> May you coil around me and teach me your secrets,
> Show me your mysteries,
> Energize my soul, and awaken my transformation within.

3. Lie down in the circle, with the pillow under your head, and close your eyes. Breathe slowly and enter a calm state. Visualize a large snake crawling from the shadows of the room and reaching your feet. Its tongue flicks at you. It slithers over your ankles, and you begin to feel a coolness extend over your body. It lifts its head and rests on top of your chest. In this position you share each other's breath.

4. Think about where you have come from and where you want to go. Envision the serpent merging into your body. Visualize a green-white light surrounding your body and slowly splitting off from you.

5. On the piece of paper, write out all that you have let go. Fold it three times and seal it with the wax from the candle on your altar. Thank the snake for sharing its wisdom and helping you shed your "skin."

6. Outside, dig a hole with the shovel and drop your piece of paper into it. Bury your past, leaving it behind you as you move forward on your rebirth.

Slaying the Psychic Vampire

Get ready to invoke your inner Buffy! Psychic vampires are energy stealers. They can usually be identified as those people who are often overly narcissistic, ego-driven, gossipy, manipulating, and jealous. In order to gain abundance and continue to manifest what you want, you need to surround yourself with people who bring you up rather than drag you down. This very simple spell involves releasing yourself from the vampires of your life and protecting against them in the future.

YOU WILL NEED:

A piece of jewelry

Elderflower oil

Bowl of black salt

Sage wand

FURTHER CONSIDERATIONS:

- **Timing:** When the waning crescent falls on a Saturday; in the planetary hour of Saturn; or when the moon is in Scorpio or Capricorn.

- **Attire:** Black.

- **Incense:** Sage.

- **Deity:** Hekate or Lilith.

- **Affirmation:** "I slay the vampires who drain me."

PERFORMING THE SPELL:

1. Select a piece of jewelry that has not already been cleansed and empowered with another form of energy. Anoint it with elderflower oil and place it into a bowl of black salt.

2. Light the sage and brush it over yourself to expel any negativity that has been attached to you. Say:

I cleanse and clear myself from the vampires who steal my energy.

3. Repeat step 2 over the bowl. Leave the bowl on a windowsill to gather the light of the waning crescent. Wear the jewelry and move forward in confidence that you are no longer attracting psychic vampires.

Transcending the Ego

Our ego has its purpose and can cultivate confidence in our lives, but it can also wreak havoc through jealousy, manipulation, and other unproductive traits. Rather than suppress the ego, it is better to transcend it. The peacock is known to symbolize nobility, dignity, and positive self-esteem, and we will utilize its essence for this spell.

YOU WILL NEED:

White cruelty-free peacock plume

Small vase

Knife

Black candle with holder

FURTHER CONSIDERATIONS:

- **Timing:** When the waning crescent falls on a Friday; in the planetary hour of Venus; or when the moon is in Libra.

- **Attire:** Black.

- **Incense:** Copal.

- **Affirmation:** "I transcend my ego."

PERFORMING THE SPELL:

1. Place the feather in the vase on your altar. Place the candleholder in front of it.

2. Carve the bottom of the candlestick so that its wick is exposed. On one side of the candle, carve your name and trace the outline with your saliva to connect it directly to you. On the other side, carve "ego."

3. Light the reversed wick. Gaze beyond the flame and into the eye of the peacock plume, saying:

> *All-seeing eye of dignity,*
> *I transcend the ego within me.*
> *Help me move beyond unproductiveness*
> *And reach a place of mental bliss.*

4. Reflect on ways your ego has gotten the best of you as the flame consumes the candle. Leave the feather on your altar and return to meditate with it in moments of need.

Witch's Ladder for Protection

A witch's ladder is another type of cord magic that is used in a variety of folk magic traditions. A cord can be designed for various reasons, such as prosperity, love, etc. However, we will make one that is designated for protection, utilizing the waning crescent's power of release to banish negativity from a space and guard against it in the future.

YOU WILL NEED:

3 black cords of equal length (the length is up to you; I'd recommend at least a foot)

9 magical items that can be any combination of the following:

OBJECT	DETAILS
Bones	Commonly found on witch's ladders. The easiest way to do this would be to clean bones from any leftover meal you've had, such as chicken.
Charms	Any charms or pendants can be added. Some ideas would be a pentacle, moons, swords, daggers, or snakes.
Crystals	Crystals like clear and smoky quartz or obsidian will aid in protection, while rose quartz will assist in bringing loving energies in.
Feathers	Feathers are very common additions to a witch's ladder. You can play around with different colors or different birds. Peacock feathers work great, as they represent the all-seeing eye of protection.
Flowers	Dried flowers, like rose, or even a thorny rose stem, would be a great symbol of protection.
Shells	These are great for people who are water signs or live next to a body of water to call upon the water spirits to protect their space.
Wood	Sticks or twigs from various trees would work well. Elder or oak are particularly strong for protection.

- **Timing:** When the waning crescent falls on a Saturday; in the planetary hour of Saturn; or when the moon is in Scorpio or Capricorn.

- **Attire:** Black.

- **Incense:** Sage or frankincense.

- **Deity:** Any.

- **Affirmation:** "My space is protected from negativity."

PERFORMING THE SPELL:

1. Gather any variation of nine objects, whether those suggested or others that you are drawn to.

2. Determine where you would like to position each object.

3. Knot the three cords together at one end with one of your objects bound by it. Repeat:

> By knot one, the spell has begun.

4. Begin to braid the cords together and anchor each remaining piece into the cord with a knot.

5. As you position and knot each object, say:

> Knot two, it will come true.
> Knot three, protect me.
> Knot four, protect this home to the core.
> Knot five, the magic comes alive.
> Knot six, enemies are nixed.
> Knot seven, this witchery is woven.
> Knot eight, security I create.
> Knot nine, this witch's ladder is mine.

6. Leave the ladder to bask in the light of the waning crescent. The next morning, hang the ladder on the back of your home's door or in a window to ward off negativity.

CONCLUSION

In Wane . . .

We've reached the end of our journey to the moon. I hope you've enjoyed the abundance of moon magic that has filled the pages of this book and that it has served as a great primer to your continued exploration of lunar mysteries. As you move forth on your magical journey with the moon, I encourage you to further research, learn, and expand your knowledge of the moon and magic in general. Let the moon be the guiding force in your life. Be the seeker and continue to grow mentally, physically, and spiritually.

As magical as the moon is, it is very important to remember that manifesting abundance is a process. If your spells and rituals are not happening as quickly as you'd like, do not fret—simply refocus and be patient. The universe does not act in accordance with our understanding of time . . . it has its own time zone! Commit to asking and to believing in the magic you are weaving. By doing so, you will ultimately receive the abundance you are after. If you are spending time worrying that your spells are not working, you are essentially putting that energy out into the world, which is counterproductive. So get out of your head and trust that everything will happen as it should, within its own time.

I recommend that you try your best to stick to the format of moon magic as described here for at least three months to reap the ultimate benefit of lunar abundance. The more you practice, the more magic will grow within you. If you have been practicing for a while, I hope that you have become inspired to work with the moon in new ways. If you are new to the craft, utilize the spells from this book as a foundation and building block to eventually write your own. The best spells you will ever work are those filled with the passion of your creation. Over time, you will find that living life to its fullest is the best spell you can cast and ultimately is the catalyst for creating abundance within your life.

In waning, thank you for allowing me the opportunity to be your tour guide on this magical journey to the moon and back. Blessed be!

MORE READING

The Door to Witchcraft — Tonya A. Brown
This is a great primer for anyone interested in dipping into the realms of modern witchcraft.

Everyday Moon Magic — Dorothy Morrison
A great guide for further exploring the magic and spells relevant to the moon's phases.

The GLAM Witch — Michael Herkes
This is my first book, which outlines my personal practice of witchcraft, anchored in the divine feminine and archetype of Lilith. It is my spiritual survival guide for finding empowerment in yourself and carving out a tradition unique to you.

Moon Magick: Myth & Magick, Crafts & Recipes, Rituals & Spells — D. J. Conway
A wonderful book that further explores the moon. The book features an array of mythology and folklore associated with the monthly moon phases.

Witch: A Magickal Journey — Fiona Horne
This was the book that helped propel me into my witch ways. Twenty years later it has withstood the test of time as a hip and inspirational guide to modern witchcraft.

Witch Way Magazine
A digital magazine devoted to many topics on witchcraft, divination, paganism, and other acts of a magical lifestyle.

REFERENCES

Buckland, R. *Buckland's Complete Book of Witchcraft*. St. Paul, MN: Llewellyn, 1986.

Cunningham, S. *Cunningham's Encyclopedia of Magical Herbs*. St. Paul, MN: Llwellyn, 2002.

Dombrowski, K. *Eight Extraordinary Days: Celebrations, Mythology, and Divination for the Witches' Wheel of the Year*. Rochester, NY: Phoebe Publishing, 2017.

Encyclopaedia Britannica. "Lunar Calender." Accessed December 17, 2019. https://www.britannica.com/science/lunar-calendar.

Grant, E. *The Book of Crystal Spells: Magical Uses for Stones, Crystals, Minerals . . . and Even Sand*. Woodbury, MN: Llewellyn, 2013.

Herkes, M. "Serpent Magic." *Witch Way Magazine,* March 2018.

Herkes, M. *The GLAM Witch: A Magical Manifesto of Empowerment with the Great Lilithian Arcane Mysteries*. Dallas, TX: Witch Way Publishing, 2019.

Horne, F. *Witch: A Magickal Journey—A Hip Guide to Modern Witchcraft*. London: Thorsons, 2000.

Morrison, D. *Everyday Moon Magic*. Woodbury, MN: Llewellyn, 2003.

Reid, L. *Moon Magic: How to Use the Moon's Phases to Inspire and Influence Your Relationships, Home Life and Business*. New York, NY: Three Rivers Press, 1998.

Resplendence.org. "The Origin of Sin and the Queen of Heaven." Accessed December 17, 2019. https://www.dhushara.com/book/orsin/origsin.htm.

Starhawk. *The Spiral Dance: A Rebirth of the Ancient Religion of the Great Goddess: 20th Anniversary Edition*. New York, NY: Harper One, 1999.

Wolfe, S. *Get Psychic!: Discover Your Hidden Powers*. New York, NY: Warner Books, 2001.

INDEX

ACKNOWLEDGMENTS

Thank you to the talented team at Callisto Media and Rockridge Press for this opportunity, particularly my editor, Lia Ottaviano, for your incredible assistance in making this book happen.

To Fiona Horne—my high priestess of positive power! You've taught me so much. Thank you for your phone calls of generous guidance, your overflowing support, and being my magical muse.

To my *Witch Way* sisters, Tonya Brown and Kiki Dombrowski—for your unconditional friendship, selflessness, and purity. Thank you for being a part of this amazing journey with me and for all of your help along the way.

To Tania Drezek, Jenni Love, Theresa Newton, and Erin VanRiper—my East Coast fairy "witch" mothers and pillars of strength, and the baddest batch of witches I know.

To my magical brother, Jesse Gillespie—for your last-minute feedback and years of friendship.

To Amara Dulcis—without whom I might have actually slept at night while writing this book. Thank you for the green absinthe and ham.

To my incredible mother, Lynne Herkes—who gave me the freedom to be the real me.

To my devoted partner, Miroslav Dulava—for loving the real me.

To my best friends, Christina Harris, Yazmin Ramos, and Kay Traylor—for being my ride or dies and never giving up on me.

To Riley Jade and Peyton Olivia—my beautiful goddess babies and moon children: The world is your oyster . . . make magic and dance in the light of the moon!

ABOUT THE AUTHOR

Michael Herkes, also known as the Glam Witch, has been practicing modern witchcraft since he was a preteen. He lives in Chicago. He is a devotee of the goddess Lilith and focuses his practice on crystal, glamour, moon, and sex magic. He is also an experienced tarot reader and has presented numerous workshops on witchcraft across the United States. Michael is the author of *The GLAM Witch* and is a regular contributor to *Witch Way Magazine*. This is his second published book. For more information, visit theglamwitch.com.

CPSIA information can be obtained
at www.ICGtesting.com
Printed in the USA
JSHW060241180922
30611JS00002B/3